Self Empowerment Reset- Our Rocky Road to Inner Peace

Rev. Dr. Marianne Padjan, Robert J. Moore, Amanda M Renaud, Jose Escobar, Julia Flynn Were, Linda McBee, Sifu Rafael Gomez, Dr. Andrea Adams-Miller, Nikki Cruise, Candice Gaddy, Tammy Williams, Cedric Singleton, Julz Vitality, Karen Hewitt, Michelle Lee, Branden McCauley, Denise Millett Burkhardt, Lulwa Saffarini

LEGAL DISCLAIMER

SELF IMPOERMENT RESET

SELF EMPOWERMENT RESET- OUR ROCKY ROAD TO INNER PEACE Copyright © 2024 MPOWERED WORD PUBLISHING. All rights reserved worldwide. No part of this material may be used, reproduced, distributed, or transmitted in any form and by any means whatsoever, including without limitation photocopying, recording or other electronic or mechanical methods or by any information storage and retrieval system, without the prior written permission from the author, except for brief excerpts in a review. This book is intended to provide general information only. Neither the author nor publisher provides any legal or other professional advice. If you need professional advice, you should seek advice from the appropriate licensed professional. This book does not provide complete information on the subject matter covered. This book is not intended to address specific requirements, either for an individual or an organization. This book is intended to be used only as a general guide, and not as a sole source of information on the subject matter. While the author has undertaken diligent efforts to ensure accuracy, there is no guarantee of accuracy or of no errors, omissions, or typographical errors. Any slights of people or organizations are unintentional. The author and publisher shall have no liability or responsibility to any person or entity and hereby disclaim all liability, including without limitation, liability for consequential damages regarding any claim, loss or damage that may be incurred, or alleged to have been incurred, directly or indirectly, arising out of the information provided in this book.

Connect with MPowered Word Publishing
www.spiritualtouch11@gmail.com

Copyright © 2024 by MPOWERED WORD PUBLISHING

All rights reserved. No part of this publication may be reproduced or transmitted in any form or by any means, electronic, or mechanical, including photocopying, recording, or by any information storage and retrieval system.

~ DEDICATIONS ~

I dedicate this book to all the people that have ever had to walk a rocky road to get to their inner peace. I want to take the time to thank you all for doing what you do to get yourself to move forward. It is not an easy Road sometimes, but it is a necessary Road for if you don't go through challenges, it is difficult to grow.

Keep growing!

Love and light!

~ Rev. Dr. Marianne Padjan

SELF IMPOERMENT RESET

~ TABLE OF COTENTS ~
CONTENTS

Foreword............Robert J. Moore............ 8

Introduction... Rev. Dr. Marianne Padjan ... 11

Chapter 1 My Rocky Road to Inner Peace... 12

Rev. Dr. Marianne Padjan

Chapter 2 ...Acceptance as a Foundation for Lasting Inner Peace............................. 21

Amanda M. Renaud

Chapter 3.... Resilient Leadership: Cultivating Joy for Next-Level Success 30

Nikki Cruise

Chapter 4 ...Driven from Fear to Glory. 35

Sifu Rafael Gomez

SELF IMPOERMENT RESET

~ TABLE OF CONTENTS ~

CONTENTS

Chapter 5 .... Perfectly Imperfect in Pursuant to Inner Peace.................................. 43

Jose Escobar

Chapter 6 ... Emotional Landscape of Entrepreneurial Leadership 47

Candice Gaddy

Chapter 7 ... Rocky Roads Are Beautiful ... 54

Tammy Williams

Chapter 8 ... Go Ahead and Look in the Mirror 59

Karen Hewitt

Chapter 9 ...From Ashes to Light 65

Julz Vitality

~ TABLE OF CONTENTS ~

CONTENTS

Chapter 10 .... The Rocky Road Brings you Success... 74

Michelle Lee

Chapter 11.... From Soldier to Salesman.... 79

Cedric Singleton

Chapter 12 ...A Dream Life Built from Leadership……..…………………………… 81

Julia Flynn Were

Chapter 13 ...The High Road; A Journey from Chaos to Conviction ………………………90

Dr. Andrea Adams-Miller

Chapter 14... The Power of Starting Over…. 96

Brendan McCauley

~ TABLE OF COTENTS ~

CONTENTS

Chapter 15 ... Finally Free.................... 103

Lulwa Saffarini

Chapter 16 .... Displayed Separation 110

Denise Millett Burkhardt

Chapter 17 ... Tools for Overcoming Life's Challenges....................................... 115

Linda McBee

Acknowledgements........................ 122

~ Foreword ~

Robert J. Moore

When I first set out on my journey, I had no idea where it would take me. All I knew was that something had to change. I was trapped in a cycle of struggle, self-doubt, and limitations that seemed to define my every step. What I've learned over the years is that the road to true leadership, personal fulfillment, and inner peace is anything but easy. It is a winding, rocky path, full of challenges, setbacks, and moments of uncertainty. But it's also a journey of profound transformation, where the toughest struggles can become the very catalysts for growth.

In Self-Empowerment: Our Rocky Road to Inner Peace, you'll find stories from other top entrepreneurs who, like me, have faced adversity head-on and come out stronger on the other side. This book isn't just about the destination; it's about the path—what it takes to break through the barriers that hold us back, to find our purpose, and to step into a life of empowered leadership.

For me, the journey began in the most difficult of circumstances—homelessness, incarceration, and a long series of personal and professional struggles. But it's those moments of despair that I learned some of my most valuable lessons. True leadership, I came to understand, isn't something you're born with. It's something you cultivate through intention, resilience, and a mindset that values long-term impact over immediate results. It's about understanding who you are, what drives you, and how to channel that energy to create meaningful change in both your personal and professional life.

SELF IMPOERMENT RESET

What I've discovered, both in my own life and in working with countless others, is that leadership begins from within. It is a journey that requires self-awareness, a willingness to confront challenges head-on, and the courage to transform obstacles into stepping stones. In my coaching practice, I've seen firsthand how the right mindset can turn adversity into opportunity, and how the simple act of showing up with passion and purpose can create a ripple effect of lasting impact. Self-Empowerment: Our Rocky Road to Inner Peace is the culmination of years of coaching, reflection, and learning. It's not just a book—it's a roadmap for anyone who wants to unlock their full potential, overcome life's challenges, and cultivate the habits and mindset that lead to sustained success. The stories in these pages are powerful reminders that success is not a straight line. It's full of detours, setbacks, and lessons that prepare us for the breakthroughs ahead.

As you read this book, I invite you to take these principles to heart. The road to true success—whether in your personal life, career, or both—will require resilience, commitment, and at times, grit. But it will also lead you to something far more valuable than material success: inner peace. That peace isn't found by avoiding the storm, but by learning how to navigate through it with clarity and confidence.

SELF IMPOERMENT RESET

I'm honored to be part of this journey alongside you. As you turn the pages of this book, my hope is that you find the inspiration, tools, and courage you need to walk your own rocky road to leadership, purpose, and peace.

Let's begin.

— Robert J. Moore

Founder of Next Level Coaching, featured in Forbes and won Guinness World Record

www.nextlevelcoaching.com

www.unlocknextlevel.com

~ Introduction ~
Rev. Dr. Marianne Padjan

This was one of the easiest books to put together out of all of my books. It really took no time at all to have all these authors to fill up the book with their remarkable stories that they all wanted to share.

The authors of this book are all entrepreneurs who have gone through the mud and come out clean. Maybe not right away clean, but eventually yes! Making the decision to become an entrepreneur is not always easy and being one is even harder at times. Whether you have been an entrepreneur for many, many years or you are brand new to it you will definitely learn and appreciate the authors as well as their chapters in this book. The readers will definitely sympathize with them as well as identify with them and therefore it will be easier for them to move forward as they understand that others have had equally as Rocky of a journey as they are also going through.

Enjoy your reading and when you're done, refer the book out to at least two struggling people you know who would benefit from reading this book.

~ Love and Light ~
Rev. Dr. Marianne Padjan

SELF IMPOERMENT RESET

~ Chapter 1 ~

Rev. Dr. Marianne Padjan

My Rocky Road to Inner Peace

My mother was barely two months pregnant when my father told her she needs to go to the clinic and get an abortion. My mother was four years old, and her mother was pregnant with her brother when her father passed away. Her mother certainly did the best she could, but she never did have a father figure ever, so she did as she was told. She did go to the clinic but once she got inside, she turned around and decided she was having this baby whether my father wanted to or not. My mother did not often show her strength, but this was one time where she was not going to budge so she told him no! He then said OKAY and married her. From what everyone else and all my family tells me they were in love always, so this was inevitable anyways all I did was speed up the journey for everybody. I had not even entered the world and already my road was Rocky. Coming into the world not wanted although I was severely loved, and I know I was no matter how abusive my father was I knew he loved me it was just an unhealthy love which I did not understand at the time I thought everybody lived this way. As I Grew Older and had friends that had different acting parents around them, I was shocked!! I had no idea the people lived in a place where their fathers not only did not hit them and abuse them but actually hug them when they came home from work and were really nice to them and ask them how they

SELF IMPOERMENT RESET

were and how their day was. I thought I was dreaming when I was at my friends house one day and we were playing on the driveway when the dad came home in a suit and (my father only wore a suit to church and weddings) he was blue collar but that was not a problem we always had everything we needed. He definitely made sure of that.

   Ask her father exited the car he came right over to her picture up gave her a big hug kiss on the cheek and she was all like disturbed because we were in this heavily playful place where she was almost upset with him because he disrupted our play time. And I thought to myself oh my gosh my father has never done that, and he would have killed me if I had ever talked to him that way. As I got older and turned into an angry teenager with way too much energy, I did get a job and then I got two jobs, and I worked overtime, and I went to school, and I did what I could to stay away from the house.

   The abuse continued and got worse the mouth ear I got the more aggressive he got, and my poor mother was in the middle. At times I would be angry because she did not leave him, why do I have to live like this? I left at sixteen and then came back and left again at 18 and came back. We then found out that my father was actually bipolar and that did not help but it did explain a few things and his aggression did not change but at least we understood some of the things he was doing and on days where he did not get much sleep and was very stressed out over pretty much anything it was really tough we did not know what to expect as he has come at me with a knife he has tried to strangle me he has hit me over my knee with a broom handle and with his extremely powerful hands as he lifted very heavy things all day so his arms were extremely powerful.

SELF IMPOERMENT RESET

All of this led to some very interesting dating and some very interesting men that I was attracted to because I had not healed enough, I was attracting very abusive men who were either abusive physically (but not to me) because I would definitely not allow that but there is different kinds of abuse there is cheating, there is emotional abuse....

My, choices as you can imagine, were questionable at best. I had given my power away many, many times. I became a people pleaser without even knowing it. I chased approval from literally everyone my bosses females, males, the guys I went out with my friends and literally everyone else in the world. I have completely lost my identity; I did not really even know who I was. I started reading books that were self empowerment self- development books, and I love them! I had no idea that I love learning about myself this much I believe this is where I learned to start loving myself. It took many years, many relationships, one marriage numerous businesses, numerous jobs a variety of different seminars, a happy mixture of coaches, living on two different continents and living through a war in Croatia. It became my full-time job and almost an addiction. Healing myself from the inside out was my soul's purpose now after many years it is my soul's purpose to help others to crawl out of the same hole that I lived in for so many years.

After hundreds of thousands of dollars and hours and hours and traveling and planes and trains and buses and cars in various parts of the world seminar after seminar after seminar I had finally earned my doctorate in metaphysics. This was my crowning Jewel to prove that I had learned to love myself finally!!! By now I had gotten divorced, we were very amicable, we just simply grew apart. We did not have any children; I did have a dog and a

SELF IMPOERMENT RESET

business. It was time to live a different style of life which came with its own challenges. If you are an entrepreneur, you already know how difficult that can get and when you are Solo, and it is just you that takes on an extra role, there were definitely plenty of ups and downs. So now I had grown quite a bit, and it was still time to continue to grow but I was repeating a lot of my same old mistakes just on a different level. Never a dull moment I was a total drama magnet. If the situation was full of ups and downs I was there. If the man was insecure, a cheater, a drug addict or alcoholic and boy oh boy if he was in jail that was the cherry on top. I sure did go out with some interesting gentleman. I most definitely did not lead a boring life.

All of this lasted another 10-15 years before I got tired of it. I wanted to change it I recognized it earlier I just couldn't. Life was so frustrating but for sure fun! I finally made a firm and conscious decision that I needed to change and so I changed my business and got a job. In search of security that I simply could not find Within Myself I got a job and a bank. A bank screams security, right? Nope!!

It was definitely different, and it was not completely drama-free, but it was different. It was the exact opposite of what I had been doing but it was still fun because it was meeting people everyday. This was a lot of fun, but the job did not pay as well as I was accustomed to, so it was never enough. While still in the field of banking I went into being a mortgage agent which was working again on straight Commission and from there I became a real estate agent and from there I left the bank, which was inevitable.

Having a real estate license was also in my opinion inevitable. I used to go for walks with my mom in the park that we live close by, and I would show her various

SELF IMPOERMENT RESET

properties that I wanted to own, and I would search Real Estate magazines endlessly looking at various properties. I was always fascinated with real estate and just felt that it was the right thing for me and that one day I would have enough money to be a real estate investor, and this would give me my Independence and my worth. You see, while I had come a long way, I was still seeking my worth outside of myself.

Well, I had finally accumulated some properties and had done pretty good for myself so much that I purchased two more properties outside of the country when times were really good. Then the real estate market shifted. It was not just the real estate market everything had shifted things were not good. I have found myself in the same place I have been years before, when I found myself having to file for bankruptcy. Well, this time it was different, yes, I was in debt, but I had properties that I could refinance. It was a similar feeling but a much different situation. My confidence level was also very different. I felt as though even if I had lost money, I would know exactly how to get it back. I was not afraid I was finally confident and believed in myself. I believed that I could and so I did!

I love my partner I love all my business partners I love what I do I love. Empowering people and making their lives better, I also love seeing happiness on my clients faces, and I love making my life better everyday. I am so happy that all of those years of reading book after book, studying course after course after course, learning, healing, crystals, various Healers, traveling to different countries, a variety of different retreats, frequency healing, drumming circles and so many more healing modalities that I can not even remember anymore. I am equally as grateful for all the negative and hard lessons that I had to go through. All of

SELF IMPOERMENT RESET

these wonderful things brought me to where I am now. It has been a heck of a journey.

Today my boundaries are tighter than ever myself worth is firmly planted in my Foundation of self-love, I am more grounded than I have ever been before and above all else I am eternally grateful for everyone and everything in my life today. I very much look forward to the rest of my beautiful life. Life is more peaceful than ever before! ~ Love and Light, Marianne

By now I had gotten divorced, we were very amicable, we just simply grew apart. We did not have any children; I did have a dog and a business. It was time to live a different style of life which came with its own challenges. If you are an entrepreneur, you already know how difficult that can get and when you are Solo and it is just you that takes on an extra role, there were definitely plenty of ups and downs. So now I had grown quite a bit, and it was still time to continue to grow but I was repeating a lot of my same old mistakes just on a different level. Never a dull moment I was a total drama magnet. If the situation was full of ups and downs I was there. If the man was insecure, a cheater, a drug addict or alcoholic and boy oh boy if he was in jail that was the cherry on top. I sure did go out with some interesting gentleman. I most definitely did not lead a boring life.

All of this lasted another 10-15 years before I got tired of it. I wanted to change it I recognized it earlier I just couldn't. Life was so frustrating but for sure fun! I finally made a firm and conscious decision that I needed to change and so I changed my business and got a job. In search of security that I simply could not find Within Myself I got a job and a bank. A bank screams security, right? Nope!!

SELF IMPOERMENT RESET

It was definitely different, and it was not completely drama-free, but it was different. It was the exact opposite of what I had been doing but it was still fun because it was meeting people everyday. This was a lot of fun, but the job did not pay as well as I was accustomed to, so it was never enough. While still in the field of banking I went into being a mortgage agent which was working again on straight Commission and from there I became a real estate agent and from there I left the bank, which was inevitable.

Having a real estate license was also in my opinion inevitable. I used to go for walks with my mom in the park that we live close by, and I would show her various properties that I wanted to own, and I would search Real Estate magazines endlessly looking at various properties. I was always fascinated with real estate and just felt that it was the right thing for me and that one day I would have enough money to be a real estate investor, and this would give me my Independence and my worth. You see, while I had come a long way, I was still seeking my worth outside of myself.

Well, I had finally accumulated some properties and had done pretty good for myself so much that I purchased two more properties outside of the country when times were really good. Then the real estate market shifted. It was not just the real estate market everything had shifted things were not good. I have found myself in the same place I have been years before, when I found myself having to file for bankruptcy. Well, this time it was different yes, I was in debt, but I had properties that I could refinance. It was a similar feeling but a much different situation. My confidence level was also very different. I felt as though even if I had lost money, I would know exactly how to get

SELF IMPOERMENT RESET

it back. I was not afraid I was finally Confident and believed in myself. I believed that I could and so I did!

I love my partner I love all my business partners I love what I do I love empowering people and making their lives better I love seeing happiness on my clients faces, and I love making my life better everyday. I am so happy that all of those years of reading book after book, studying course after course, after course learning, healing, crystals, various Healers, traveling to different countries, a variety of different retreats, frequency healing, drumming circles and so many more healing modalities that I can; t even remember anymore. I am equally as grateful for all the negative and hard lessons that I had to go through. All of these wonderful things brought me to where I am now. It has been a heck of a journey.

Today my boundaries are tighter than ever myself worth is firmly planted in my Foundation of self-love, I am more grounded than I have ever been before and above all else I am eternally grateful for everyone and everything in my life today. I very much look forward to the rest of my beautiful life. Life is more peaceful than ever before!

~ **Love and Light** ~

Rev. Dr. Marianne Padjan

SELF IMPOERMENT RESET

~ Contact Rev. Dr. Marianne Padjan ~

http://sites.google.com/view/mariannepadjan594029/home

http://codebreakerglobal.com/crackyourcode/marilove

http://m.facebook.com/Marianne.padjan?wtsid=rdr_0WfKlvKxFMRi7Pf

~ Chapter 2 ~
Amanda M. Renaud
Acceptance As a Foundation for Lasting Inner Peace

When we think of peace, many thoughts come to mind, many ideologies and many desires also arise. Some say peace is a state of mind, and some believe it is something you work towards and build. For me —it has always been a bit of both. One thing I do know for certain is that peace comes from within, it comes from the way you think, how you respond, and how you choose to conquer the world around you. It requires constant internal reflection and a strong sense of philosophy to really come to peace with anything we may stumble upon in our lives. Peace comes from our ability to leverage our life experiences with acceptance, compassion, and awareness.

Many times, in my own personal life, I was forced to find some level of peace and rebuild my entire life. When I speak of finding peace, it's merely a state of existence where your soul, being, spirit, and mind can accept elements or changing circumstances our lives. See — chaos can come from discomfort, change, and unpredictability. Chaos and its perception for many individuals is often different for everyone. One commonality I do find is that it causes pain and suffering for all. In order to achieve peace, one must be ready to stand in the cyclone of chaos and

SELF IMPOERMENT RESET

really have the courage enough to explore that chaos and discomfort. Peace does not mean everything goes our way, and everything is perfect. Sometimes, peace looks like a finale to a cruel season of life. Sometimes, it looks like compromise, acceptance, or even understanding.

Peace starts with a foundation of self- awareness, growth, and acceptance. Peace is maintained with time, perseverance, and reframing the way you see and experience life. Like anything in life, a cycle of changing circumstances with every second, minute, and hour of the day. You will not find peace in environments that created chaos or despair for you. You will not find peace in toxicity or negativity. From my own experience, it was only when I was honest about my own progress that the people around me and the actions I was or was not taking. People often assume peace comes from trivial things such as love, money, achievements, and vanity. These things can contribute to overall happiness or can be tools such as — money.

However, peace looks like happiness, composure, and humility on the outside, but the inside often feels like calmness, clarity, and the absence of invasive thoughts or enemies. Invasive thoughts often come out as destructive or negative behaviors. Let us never forget that behavior IS a language and a good metric in determining if you have in fact, made peace with a circumstance. A lot of individuals forget that reactivity does not equal productivity, nor will it bring peace. Peace can only be achieved when you are ready to accept the circumstances, ploy solutions, and strategies, and find a way to accept what is.

Many want instant gratification, and sometimes, it is just not possible. The ability to look at a problem and decide if

SELF IMPOERMENT RESET

it is one you can solve on your own or if it requires time, others, and patience is a huge piece of the puzzle to finding true inner peace. Sometimes, all you have with some circumstance — is time. How you choose to use that time will be what will lead to peace and happiness. As someone who spent fifteen years in litigation, there were many days I was my own worst enemy. I felt I had no control over my life, and perhaps it was partially true. The only thing I could control was my reactions. Your peace comes from your ability to be patient and to have trust in yourself. When you're experiencing turmoil and problematic situations, sometimes no reaction at all will bring you peace. Not every situation deserves a response.

In order to be at peace, your resilience must be stronger than your lack of faith. The consequences of being reactive to every misfortune can be the absence of peace and healthy relationships because people under pressure or stress can fold, crack, and be confrontational. Much of what we react to because of others —is not about us. Its about their war with themselves and learning not to own their issues will bring you peace. Understanding that you can not control others or everything happening around you also brings peace. You can only control yourself and YOUR response. If you choose to attend every battle you're invited to, life will be stressful, and an absence of peace will be prominent. Peace is something everyone seeks, but few know how to maintain or nourish, and so we as a collective are always searching for peace, and often when we experience it —we do not appreciate it.

Often, we skip past the most peaceful days and forget to give gratitude to them. Life works like a domino effect. If we choose to ignore problems in our lives, it simply means it's a growing problem. Growing problems begin to cause

SELF IMPOERMENT RESET

ripples in other areas of our lives, and suddenly, we are standing in front of the mirror or others, wondering how it got to this point. We must be swift and quick in creating stability and order from misfortune. If we choose to dwell on problems or emotions, we lose the ability to be rational and realistic and hit that problem head-on. Never let any problem intimidate you or make you fold. Keep going! The problems we as individuals face must never be left to sort themselves out because we miss the opportunity to do some real inner work and grow. A problem with a reactive emotional response to a situation is a good indicator that there is inner work to do, and that's where you master inner peace. Learning to identify where the work needs to be done. Peace does not come from your ability to ignore circumstances or problems always. It comes from how quickly you can recover and control your emotional responses and implement strategies that fuel your drive and make you feel good.

Again, reactivity does equal productivity nor peace! We often can let emotions take the lead and respond full of emotion, and sensationalized responses do not mean a solution or understanding has or will come to fruition. I once knew a really loud person who thought talking things out required yelling and cursing to get their point across. This made me uncomfortable on every level. It did nothing for me as the listener— other than shut me down. I heard when I was younger. " The loudest person in the room is usually the one who was never heard as a child." It always stuck in my mind. This person wanted to be heard, but yelling was not going to work for me. It turned into me cutting them off completely because I could not handle the aggressive, loud nature. We all have limits and boundaries, and when they are crossed, we can surely shut down and lose the entirety of the message the other person is trying

SELF IMPOERMENT RESET

to get out. Peace means our communication is clear and concise, and we say yes to the things we want and no to the things we do not want. Listening to our minds and souls and spirits is a crucial part of peace. You can not go to war with yourself in the name of love for others! You will lose yourself. You will lose and create the opposite of inner peace. If it makes you uncomfortable or hurts, it's just the way it is. Be accountable for your own feelings, reactions, and emotions and enforce that within your relationships. You will not find yourself amidst chaos nor peace. Peace comes from building a strong foundation of boundaries, acceptance, and most importantly, understanding self. Understanding how you move under pressure or conflict and having an awareness of the people and environments around you is also important. Understanding your own limitations and who you are and as well as your own level of tolerance will bring you much inner peace. Peace does not come from places, belongings, or possessions.

    A societal misconception many may think is that; lavish materials and vacations equate peace—not true. Building a life you don't need vacations from is real peace. When you can wake up in the morning with gratitude, love, and happiness in your heart— that is peace! One must remember that life is a continual cycle of change, problems, hurdles and loss, and struggles are also a part of that journey. It is what we find within ourselves the knowledge, experience, and growth that comes from all of it —that leads to peace. Peace is not something that you can buy, fake, or embellish. It is the most sought-after state of life. We all want that for ourselves, but few are willing to do the work to get to that state of mind. Myself, I have been guilty more times than not in being reactive and making a problem worse, leading to chaos, especially in my younger

SELF IMPOERMENT RESET

years. With hard work, commitment, self-awareness, and acceptance, you CAN find peace within.

An individual must be courageous, honest, and dedicated to finding peace. Anytime a person, place, or situation brings turmoil and chaos, you must be able to cut it off. Be ready to implement strategy to ground yourself, your mind, body, and soul. This is not to be confused with discomfort because discomfort brings growth and a deeper insight and understanding into ourselves and the world, we are experiencing around us. Every time you handle discomfort and pain, one must view it as a new journey that they will conquer and grow from. We often associate misfortune, anger, and negative emotions as something bad, and so we often choose to sweep it under the rug and let it dominate it. Even the negative experiences should be embraced, not to hold on to torture ours minds with, but rather to learn from and reframe. When we make a conscious decision to reframe our experiences as something that makes sense to us, we can begin to accept it as a part of a necessary part of the cycles and seasons of life, we begin to realize what a sense of internal peace is. Of course, life will always have tragedy that makes no sense and is just awful to experience at all levels. Time will be the biggest healer and guide to inner peace. Accepting that time is continual and forever changing, and it has the ability to bring forth just as much success, peace, and grace —but you have to stay!

All those moments that are painful, lonely, disappointing, and full of sorrow —own them., feel them, embrace them, and experience them however you need to. Never forget it will pass, and you will find that light and peace within. You find peace within when you give yourself grace, patience, and time. Others can offer peace to you by modeling the same. Individuals who give you that grace,

SELF IMPOERMENT RESET

time, and patience will always be special individuals who should be cherished. In fact, some of these authors in this very book have changed my life and shown me what peace can look like. When the pages of your story no longer cause you distress and you can talk about it without anger, regret, or despair, that is what inner peace is. May we always strive for it, offer it to others, and work towards it. May our hearts be ready and steadfast, may our words heal rather than hurt, and may our hearts offer peace and comfort always in all we do. It is with time, acceptance, grace, and humility that we find inner peace.

It is with unconditional love we give to ourselves and others that we find peace, joy, and happiness. Time and growth have the power to change our circumstances, but one but always consider their responsibilities regardless. Many people admire peace and nature and its divine connection because it merely exists in all its beauty, and that is what we must strive toward. Accepting that all the seasons of life serve a purpose, and it is our character and how we show up to steadfast the seasons that can bring us peace. Our presence and the way we choose to show up can either fuel a season leading to growth, or we can hinder our own journey, straying off the course from time to time—but always keep going!

— Amanda M. Renaud

SELF IMPOERMENT RESET

~ Amanda M. Renaud ~

Amanda is an Experienced Leader with a demonstrated history of working in Sales, leadership, and Entrepreneurship for more than twenty years. Amanda is the CEO of Magnetic Entrepreneur Inc. founded by Robert J. Moore. Magnetic Entrepreneur is A globally recognised publishing Brand featured In Forbes, yahoo finance and USA today. Magnetic Entrepreneur Inc also holds a Guiness World Record and won the Global Recognition award of 2023 for their continued publishing and coaching services. Magnetic Entrepreneur Founded by Robert J Moore a New Times Best selling Author and huge Inspiration to Amanda for many years. Amanda a 6x International Best-Selling Author herself. Amanda continues to make her impact in the publishing world, while carrying on Robert's legacy. Amanda holds an Advanced Diploma in Child and Youth treatment and has knowledge in Program development, Community services, Crisis Intervention, Business Development, and Customer Relationship Management (CRM). Amanda is a Strong professional who is also a certified life coach and has won numerous Awards in Canada for sales and her writing. Amanda is a motor vehicle accident survivor who has made immense impact for her herself and the people around her. Amanda has transformed her life into the true definition of success. Amanda also released her first Solo Self development Novel in October of 2023 " Exceptional Minds" a wonderful prelude into her Leadership teachings and upcoming course designed to enhance leadership skills

SELF IMPOERMENT RESET

globally. Amanda also became a number one best seller just recently with her newest co-authorship book Luminous Leaders where herself and co- authors share valuable knowledge about leadership. Amanda was presented with a lifetime achievement award recently for her continued work in publishing and contributions to leadership from the Mind Academy Arena. Amanda continues to focus on serving others, provide quality publishing, and coaching services that are empowering the lives of many globally. Amanda a single mother of three sons who has faced many hardships throughout her life but despite the challenges, she continues to share her knowledge and help emerging writers face the challenges in publishing and everyday life with her diverse skill set and continued efforts driven by her compassion for writing and serving the people around her.

Magneticpublishing2023@gmail.com

www.magnetic-entrepreneur.com

SELF IMPOERMENT RESET

~ Chapter 3 ~

Nikki Cruise

Resilient Leadership: Cultivating Joy for Next-Level Success

Introduction

- **Opening Story:**
  In 2020, a global survey revealed that 60% of leaders felt more isolated and overwhelmed than ever before. Pressure to perform, innovate, and lead through crises has never been higher. I've been there leading through adversity while questioning my own capacity to keep going. But one realization changed everything: resilience isn't just about bouncing back; it's about thriving joyfully in the face of challenges.

- **Introduction of Resilience as Core:**
  Leadership today demands more than skills; it requires a resilient spirit that can weather storms while inspiring others. Resilience isn't a fallback—it's a strategy for sustainable, joyful leadership.

- **Compelling Question:**
  "What if resilience wasn't just about surviving **but** thriving joyfully, even in the hardest seasons? What would that look like for you, your team, and your mission?"

SELF IMPOERMENT RESET

Section 1: The Power of Resilient Leadership

- **Defining Resilient Leadership:**
  Resilient leadership is the ability to adapt, lead with clarity, and inspire others during uncertain times. It's about maintaining focus and influence while embodying unwavering integrity.

- **The Unique Challenges of CLA Leaders:**
  As CLA members, you're at the forefront of global influence, often balancing growth with authenticity. Resilience ensures you can navigate these challenges without losing sight of your vision or values.

- **Key Insight:**
  Resilient leaders inspire trust and innovation. They show others that leadership is not about perfection but progress, clarity, and joy in the journey.

Biblical Reference:
"Not only that, but we rejoice in our sufferings, knowing that suffering produces endurance, and endurance produces character, and character produces hope." — *Romans 5:3-4*

Section 2: Why Joy Matters in Leadership

- **The Neuroscience of Joy:**
  Studies show that joy releases dopamine and serotonin, enhancing creativity, problem-solving, and motivation. Joy isn't just a "feel-good" emotion; it's a leadership tool that fuels long-term success.

SELF IMPOERMENT RESET

- **Impact on Team Dynamics:**
  Joyful leaders foster environments of collaboration and trust. When leaders prioritize joy, team morale soars, and performance follows.

- **Transformative Story:**
  A leader I worked with was drowning in stress, leading a team under immense pressure. By shifting her focus to celebrating small wins and practicing gratitude, her outlook—and her team's output—transformed.

Interactive Moment:
Reflect on a recent challenge you faced. Now, think about one moment during that challenge where choosing joy could have shifted your mindset or outcome.

Biblical Reference:
"The joy of the Lord is your strength." — *Nehemiah 8:10*

Section 3: Strategies to Cultivate Joyful Resilience

1. Mindset Mastery

- Reframe setbacks as opportunities for growth.

- Shift from "What's going wrong?" to "What can I learn from this?"

- **Practical Tip:** Start each day with a "growth question," such as: "How can I use today's challenges to grow stronger as a leader?"

2. Authentic Leadership

- Stay true to your core values, even under pressure.

- **Quick Exercise:** Take a moment to write down one value you want to embody every day as a leader.

SELF IMPOERMENT RESET

3. The Joy Practice

- Develop daily habits that cultivate joy:
    - Gratitude journaling—write three things you're grateful for each morning.
    - Celebrate small wins with your team, recognizing progress over perfection.
    - Prioritize well-being through consistent rest and spiritual renewal.
- Embed joy into your team dynamics: Begin meetings by sharing "joy moments" to set a positive tone.

Section 4: Next-Level Success Through Resilient Leadership

- **Joy and Resilience Fuel Growth:**
  Resilience without joy leads to burnout; joy without resilience lacks direction. Together, they create sustainable momentum for high-level leadership.

- **Align Leadership with Purpose:**
  Your success as a leader is not just in outcomes but in leading with authenticity, clarity, and joy. When your leadership aligns with your purpose, it elevates your impact exponentially.

- **Application for CLA Leaders:**
  These principles equip you to lead in industries and global contexts while staying anchored in your values and mission.

Call-to-Action:
"What steps will you take to lead with joy and resilience starting today? Your next level of success—and your team's—is waiting."

SELF IMPOERMENT RESET

Conclusion

- **Quote:**
  "Leadership is not about being in charge. It is about taking care of those in your charge." — Simon Sinek

- **Reiterate Transformative Power:**
  Resilient leadership is the foundation of lasting impact. When cultivated with joy, it becomes the key to thriving in every season and challenge.

- **Final Reflection:**
  As you leave today, I invite you to reflect on your unique leadership journey. How will you embrace resilience, anchored in joy, to inspire others and drive meaningful success?

Final Biblical Reference:
"Whatever you do, work heartily, as for the Lord and not for men." — *Colossians 3:23*

This message is designed to empower entrepreneurial leaders to see resilience not as a fallback but as a strategy that aligns with their values and fuels their impact.

SELF IMPOERMENT RESET

~ Nikki Cruise ~

Nikki Cruise is an energetic and dynamic international TEDx speaker, bestselling author, and empowerment coach, who in sharing her miraculous testimony brings hope and encouragement in the healing power of joy. The joy that brought about her healing of body, mind, and spirit.

As a coach, she encourages women to recognize their own value, regardless of the circumstances and society's inevitable labels, so that they can see how to powerfully impact the world through their unique calling and purpose through her J.U.M.P.P. program. (Joyfully Unleashing a More Powerful Purpose)
She empowers leaders in business to excel in their leadership, implement strategies and be equipped with tools to daily choose abundance and joy, seeking out solutions to adversity in all circumstances and leading others to do the same.

Nikki, originally from South Africa, resides in Burleson, Texas, USA.

Links
https://www.facebook.com/nikki.cruise.7

https://www.linkedin.com/in/nikkijoyinspired

Website: www.joy-inspired.com

~ Chapter 4 ~

Sifu Rafael Gomez

Driven From Fear to Glory

Life doesn't wait for permission before teaching its lessons. It strikes with force—sometimes with joy, sometimes with agony—but always with purpose. Through each trial, we are given the tools to reshape ourselves, to confront our past and decide who we will become. This is one of many stories that have shaped who I have become—one of fear, resilience, and ultimately, glory. It's about finding strength in the darkest places, discovering forgiveness where there was once only pain, and learning that even in the toughest of times, we are never beyond redemption.

Childhood and Early Challenges

By the time I was ten, I had already been molded by a world of chaos and violence that I had come to accept as normal. Self-blame was my constant companion. Each day, I carried the weight of wondering why I had become someone's punching bag, why the pain felt so unavoidable. It was a heavy burden for someone so young. One morning, I woke to a sudden shock—a yank on my blanket, leaving me exposed to the morning cold. Before I could even fully open my eyes, a sharp lash cut through the air. It was a washing machine hose, wielded by my mother with force I never imagined. The shock sent me twisting, scrambling to shield myself, but the blows came relentlessly, burning my skin, cutting into me like fire. I hadn't known that asking for a little money would trigger this. "We are not beggars, and you will never ask for money again!" Her voice was as cold as the air, each word punctuated by another strike. And I learned that day—a lesson that scarred me deeper than the blows themselves—that I would never ask for anything again.

Moving to the United States

Just when I thought I couldn't endure any more, life shifted unexpectedly. My parents decided to move us from Colombia to the United States. First, my father left. Then, my mother followed, and we were scattered among relatives in Colombia until they settled. I went to live with my older sister Rosa and her husband Guillermo, who welcomed me into their home with warmth I hadn't known. Their house was large and peaceful—a stark contrast to the constant tension I'd known. And for the first time in my life, the beatings stopped. Still, a part of me remained uneasy. I couldn't fully accept this new calm, as though I was waiting for the other shoe to drop. Without the daily violence, I felt... lost. There were days I would bang my head against the wall in frustration, trying to make sense of a life without fear. It was as though I missed the chaos. It was the only thing my mind knew.

In March of 1973, just days before my eighth birthday, my parents sent for us to join them in Jackson Heights, New York. The promise of a new life—one filled with freedom—made my heart race. But that promise was short-lived. Being back with my parents meant the beatings began again, but with even more fury. My father would chase me through the house, whipping me with his belt, the buckle tearing into my skin. My mother, too, would lash out with anything within reach, her hands leaving bruises I couldn't hide. When someone at school noticed the marks and asked about them, my mother claimed it was dirt, explaining I "refused to shower." So, I stopped showering—to make her lie true.

Finding Independence

At ten, I started secretly working. No one knew where I went or what I did. I was the tenth of twelve children, a shadow among my siblings. No one questioned where I was during those hours. I took a job cleaning a bingo hall, earning cash without anyone's approval. The feeling of that first payment, held tightly in my hand, was intoxicating. For the first time, I didn't have to ask anyone for anything. And most importantly, no one could punish me for it.

My work ethic caught the eye of a Greek man named George. He had side businesses in abundance—selling shish kebabs, shaved ice, helping with roofing—and he paid me cash. I learned that if I kept quiet and worked hard, I could earn money on my own terms. With George, I found a strange sense of freedom. He never asked my age, never questioned my background. To him, I was just a worker, and for a brief moment, I felt like I could escape the past.

Moments of Defiance

Also, at the age of ten, I made a decision that would change everything. I refused to live in fear any longer. One day, without a word to anyone, I gathered a few belongings, took some money, and ran away. My only friend—my confidante—was the only person who knew, and he promised to keep my secret. That first night, I slept in a stranger's backyard, hidden in the bushes, the cold

SELF IMPOERMENT RESET

grass beneath me my only comfort. For the next two weeks, I lived like a ghost, roaming the streets, taking food when I could, and avoiding detection. At one point, I saw my older brother Cesar, riding his bike and calling out my name, searching for me. I hid behind parked cars, my heart racing as I watched him pass by. He didn't find me, but the fact that he was looking gave me a strange sense of comfort.

Eventually, hunger and exhaustion caught up with me. I ended up at my friend's house, grateful for a warm meal. But his mother had already called my family. Before I knew it, they had arrived to drag me back home. The moment I stepped through the door, I was met with a beating fiercer than any before. But it didn't matter. I had made my stand. I had run away, and for the first time, I had tasted freedom.

A Moment of Change

Then came the day when everything changed. My father tried to strike me again, but this time, I didn't run. I didn't cower. I stood my ground, as still as a statue, refusing to give him the satisfaction of seeing me afraid. His fury was palpable, but so was my resolve. His eyes widened with shock as he realized he wasn't facing a frightened child anymore—he was facing someone who had found strength in the face of his terror. I stood there, silent, unflinching. And slowly, his anger turned to confusion. Eventually, he stopped. He was exhausted, unable to break me. That day, something inside him changed too—he never raised a hand to me again. But the battle wasn't over. My mother, too, would try to break me. One day, she attacked me with a stick. But this time, I didn't flinch. I blocked her blows with my arm, refusing to be the victim her with the weapon.

SELF IMPOERMENT RESET

Her face twisted in rage, but she didn't take the knife. Instead, she hissed through gritted teeth, "No, I don't want to take you out you now, I will do it slowly." Those words stung more than any blow and the look in her eyes was the most terrifying I had ever seen on her. That was the last time she ever laid a hand on me.

A New Chapter

The lashings stopped, and my parents, unable to control me, decided to send me to a youth home. But I had already made a plan. I would run away again, far from everyone. Then, just when I least expected it, God intervened. My sister Rosa and her husband Guillermo stepped in, offering to take me in and let me live with them. They saved me once again, and that's where I truly began to heal. It took me a long time—eight years, in fact—to forgive my parents. When I was 18, I was ready to sever ties with my entire family, except for Rosa and Guillermo, who had become my angels. I didn't want to hear what anyone else had to say, but my sister's tears made me reconsider. She asked me to think it over for a week, and I agreed. After praying about it, I realized she was right.

Forgiveness starts with me. I realized that I could forgive my parents without needing them to accept or acknowledge it. It was a powerful lesson. I learned that forgiveness doesn't require reconciliation, and I don't have to be a victim anymore. I never raised my hand against my children. Instead, I make sure they feel loved every single day. As I was drafting this story, I paused to call my sons and tell them how much I love them.

SELF IMPOERMENT RESET

My message to you: Take charge of the voices in your mind. You hold the power to speak to yourself and others with kindness and love—make it a daily practice. May you be blessed with peace, love, and an amazing life.

— **Sifu Rafael Gomez**

SELF IMPOERMENT RESET

~ Sifu Rafael Gomez ~

Sifu Rafael is a Master instructor and the Founder of Speaking Prowess, where he combines expertise in communication and leadership to help individuals unlock their full potential. As a public speaker, solutions expert, and executive coach, Sifu Rafael leverages years of experience to guide clients towards their goals with clarity, purpose, and strategic insight. His mission is to make the art of effective communication accessible to all, empowering personal and professional growth. Sifu Rafael's unwavering dedication to improving communication skills has earned him a reputation as a trusted mentor and coach. His vision is clear: to enhance communication worldwide, one individual at a time.

https://sifurafael.com/

https://www.facebook.com/SifuRafaelG/

https://www.youtube.com/@sifurafaeltv

~ Chapter 5 ~

Jose Escobar

Perfectly Imperfect in Pursuit of Inner Peace

There is a famous quote that states "inner peace begins the moment you choose not to allow another person or event to control your emotions." I'm sure this idea will resonate with you on some level, and my hope is that this chapter will shed some light not only on the importance of inner peace but also how to acquire it. There is no doubt that the pursuit of being at peace in your heart is a non-linear journey with many ebbs and flows, highs and lows, and peaks and valleys. I always like to say that in order to reach the promised land, you have to go through the city dump. Achieving inner peace is a challenge worth embracing. Many people set out to achieve it, yet they become frustrated because the peace they seek can be as elusive as the pot of gold at the end of the rainbow.

In order to find it, you can't simply rely on your desire or persistence. You need some tools to turn to when the going gets tough. What exactly is inner peace? It's safe to say that inner peace is a state of contentment and joy in your heart in the midst of life's challenges. We don't achieve inner peace with the absence of the challenges. It's more of a process of knowing how to effectively manage the external circumstances so that our interior life can be at ease. Let's be clear about what inner peace is not.

SELF IMPOERMENT RESET

Inner peace is not the absence of difficulty. It is also not passive. Things need to happen in order for inner peace to happen. There is always something more to do, so it's important to be aware that seeking inner peace is a continual process. Inner peace also does not mean isolation from the world. And it certainly isn't something that you get from a specific person. Achieving inner peace is a must in order for us to thrive personally and professionally. There are many benefits to finding that inner peace we all seek. For example, better sleep, improved mood, boost in confidence, lower levels of stress and anxiety, and improved relationships. As you can see, inner peace makes our own life better, and it also improves how we relate to others around us.

The road is most certainly rocky in pursuit of inner peace. Our daily lives can be sources of anxiety and stress as we struggle to balance the demands of family life, work, and everything else. It's not easy being a committed spouse, loving parent, and dedicated professional, all while still taking care of your health. We have the stressors of meeting our career goals, the pressure of performing based off of quotas, goals, and metrics. Perhaps there are past traumas that have impacted us in a negative way. For example, growing up in a broken home, physical, verbal, or sexual abuse, growing up in poverty, exposure to violence at a young age, tough relationship break ups, etc. These are wounds that are frequently carried into adulthood that inevitably can lead to divorce, being an absent parent, drug and alcohol abuse, financial ruin, bankruptcy, eviction, car repossession, broken familiar relationships, poor health, and can even ruin your relationship with your Creator, God. There is no scarcity of stressors in our modern lives. Welcome to being a human being with a pulse.

SELF IMPOERMENT RESET

If we're not careful, we can be a source of our own internal turmoil if we do not take our thoughts captive. We may not necessarily be in control of the thoughts that come into our mind, but we certainly have control over the thoughts we choose to entertain and let linger in our mind that can ultimately create a stronghold. How do you talk to yourself internally? Common negative self talk could sound like this: "I don't think I can do this anymore," "I'm not good enough," "if only I were (thinner, smarter, funnier, etc.)," "this is too hard for me," "I'm never going to be like…." It is vital that we remain vigilant and self aware of what we say to ourselves on a regular basis. Remember, the subconscious mind never sleeps, and it accepts all statements as true even if consciously you know it is not true. A very simple practice is to turn the negative thought on its head and find the opposing positive thought to replace it with. For example, instead of thinking "this is too hard for me," say to yourself "I can do hard things, and I'm ready, willing, and able to learn."

Embracing imperfection is undoubtedly a concept we must accept. We are all flawed and imperfect no matter how hard we try to pursue perfection, it is just not possible. The sooner you embrace this reality, the faster your pace will be to achieve inner peace. Additionally, there are many practical things you can do on a daily basis to support your journey. Finding time to pray is essential to weathering the external storms of life without becoming anxious. Meditation and spending time in stillness and quiet is also an important piece of the puzzle, especially when trying to hear God's voice speaking to you. Some may call it mindfulness, but I like to call it prayer and meditation. The quest for inner peace, in my opinion, essentially boils down to having holes in our heart that need to be filled. As

SELF IMPOERMENT RESET

author Matthew Kelly likes to say, "the holes in our heart are God sized holes."

Another important aspect to consider is that inner peace is not found instantaneously. It does not come overnight, and we must be patient. As Aristotle notably said, "patience is bitter, but its fruit is sweet." Another memorable quote worth mentioning is one by Leo Tolstoy. He says that "the two most powerful warriors are patience and time." If we allow ourselves to accept the wait, we will have matured over time, just like a diamond starts off as a piece of coal, the end is worthwhile. There will be roadblocks, there will be detours, there will be speedbumps, but we must push through it all and not become discouraged. There is tremendous power in reframing your thoughts, as stated earlier, seeking support from those closest to you, and adjusting your expectations as you progress.

As you search for peace, mistakes will be made along the way. Don't look at this as a dead end or waste of time. Failure is a part of the process, as long as you are failing forward and learning from your mistakes. It's been said countless times that if you fall down seven times, you get up eight. How true is that? My encouragement to you is to pursue inner peace relentlessly despite how hard it may seem at times. It is worth the effort and without question will lead to a personal transformation unlike anything you've ever experienced. There is work to do, and you must be willing to put in the work. The reality is that most people do not. I believe in you and trust you will lean into this process starting today with a renewed vigor and conviction. You deserve to have inner peace, and those closest to you deserve the best version of you.

SELF IMPOERMENT RESET

~ Jose Escobar ~

Jose Escobar, an acclaimed personal development speaker and 10x published author, leads two successful businesses: The Entrepreneur's Bookshelf and the Connected Leaders Academy that has surpassed over 7-figures in 15 months organically. He engages with entrepreneurs and advanced leaders, collectively reaching over 30 million through presentations and coaching programs. He works with over 350 successful leaders globally. Jose is a master sales professional. He is happily married with 5 kids. Discover more about Jose's offerings at:

www.ConnectedLeadersAcademy.com

~ Chapter 6 ~
Candice Gaddy
Emotional Landscape of Entrepreneurial Leadership

I do not know about you, but I never planned to be an entrepreneur when I grew up! Now as I look back, I cannot believe I never saw this as an option. Maybe because I had never personally known a successful entrepreneur. I know why now because this is not for the faint at heart. I decided I was going to become a finance executive because I was so good at numbers! I went on to lead some of the most well-known companies in the world. I checked every box I had created for myself until life hit, altering my health for the rest of my life with a stroke and brain hemorrhage. Even then I was committed to my career, but I had to make some hard decisions when I was laid off and forced to deal with the reality that regardless of my strong skillsets, I am dispensable given I had no ownership of the vision and direction! I was simply a contributing member to helping someone else realize their own.

That is when I made the hard decision to "Never Be Unplugged again" I would leverage my skills I poured into others to create my own freedom on my own terms. It all sounds good until you must walk the journey out or not feed your children. It is just that journey and boy o boy is that journey rocky. No one tells you how hard the road is for leaders! It is a conscious decision every day to stay on

SELF IMPOERMENT RESET

the road and not give in to what may appear to be an easier route or on some days jump off the cliff. The emotional landscape of being an entrepreneur can be both deeply rewarding and challenging. This journey is often shaped by the intersection of personal growth, professional development, and the nurturing of others, which requires emotional resilience, and self-awareness.

Empathy and Compassion.

As an entrepreneur, you likely feel a profound sense of empathy for others and their struggles. Your work is driven by a deep desire to help, guide, and support people on their journey. This can create an emotional connection with clients or customers, leaving you with a sense of fulfillment when you see their transformation or growth. Sharing your personal healing story or the journey that led you to entrepreneurship often requires vulnerability. This can be liberating, as it allows you to connect with others who may be on similar paths. Many times, this results in narrowing down your niche or whom you want to work with daily. That alone can add to another layer of stress.

It can also bring moments of insecurity or fear of judgment, especially when you expose parts of yourself that are still healing or trying to figure out. The emotional work of showing up authentically is ongoing and can sometimes feel overwhelming. Imposter Syndrome and Self Doubt Despite your expertise, entrepreneurs often grapple with imposter syndrome—feeling like they are not good enough or that they are not truly deserving of success. This emotional challenge can be even more pronounced for women, as societal expectations around gender and leadership can lead to added pressure and self-doubt. As a mom of two very active boys I live it every day. Do I work

SELF IMPOERMENT RESET

later today to make sure the client who is paying me has what they need so I can go to my sons game tomorrow?

Every day is a juggle, there is no copy paste answer. You figure it all out while on the rocky road to success. While learning from the past, CHOOSING to be present in the moment, and planning for the future! You MUST remind yourself daily of how amazing you are and do not forget the wins you already have. Many are too busy looking at the mountain ahead that you forget the valley you just climbed out of! On the other hand, as you continue to grow your business and gain clients, there is a sense of validation that slowly pushes back against these feelings of inadequacy, creating a wave of confidence and pride.

Empowerment and Independence

Running your own business can be empowering. You have the autonomy to create something that aligns with your values and passions. This independence can create feelings of joy and personal achievement. The tricky part is realizing you work for yourself and your clients at the same time. The illusion of complete freedom many seek and desire outside looking in is soon wiped away with the reality that soon smacks you in the face. Yet, with this power comes the weight of responsibility. There is often a fine line between independence and isolation, as you juggle the demands of entrepreneurship, such as finances, marketing, and business decisions, while still holding space for clients, emotional needs.

Uncertainty and Fear

Like all entrepreneurs, you often face uncertainty—whether its financial instability, market changes, or personal fears about success and failure. These moments of fear can trigger anxiety or self-doubt, at the same time, there is an underlying hope and belief in the work you are doing. These challenges can fuel growth and resilience, making the emotional landscape feel like a constant dance between fear and hope, struggle, and breakthrough.

Joy and Gratitude

One of the most rewarding aspects is seeing the positive impact your work has on others. Witnessing clients transform, heal, or grow often evokes profound joy and gratitude. These moments of success—big or small—are emotionally fulfilling and provide the energy needed to continue your work, even when the road gets tough.

Connection and Community

Many entrepreneurs find strength in the sense of community they build—whether. Through their clients, support networks, or fellow entrepreneurs. This sense of connection can be a source of emotional support, encouragement, and shared wisdom. Still, there are times when loneliness can creep in, particularly in the early stages of entrepreneurship, or when you are navigating challenges that feel isolating.

Self-Care and Balance

A crucial emotional challenge for entrepreneurs is learning to prioritize their own well-being. The very nature of your work requires giving, which can sometimes lead to neglecting your own needs. Finding balance between your professional life and self-care is essential, as burnout can hinder your ability to serve others. This ongoing dance between service and self-care can stir up feelings of guilt, especially when you feel torn between personal needs and

SELF IMPOERMENT RESET

the demands of your business. I found freedom one random day at a networking event when a speaker told me "Candice you will NEVER find balance," Rather "learn to prioritize and dance to your own rhythm"! Life presents the unknown no matter how much we plan! Give yourself the grace and agility to be flexible just like you are to the people you lead!

Conclusion

Being an entrepreneur is an emotional journey full of highs and lows. The rewards come from helping others, the freedom of owning a business, and the personal growth that comes with being both a healer and an entrepreneur. However, challenges like self- doubt, vulnerability, emotional burnout, and fear of failure can make the road feel uncertain. The key lies in cultivating self-compassion, setting boundaries, and staying connected to both your inner healing and the support of a nurturing community.

SELF IMPOERMENT RESET

~ Candice Gaddy ~

Candice Gaddy is a continual Life Learner. She holds a bachelor's degree in finance, licensed certified international coach, master's in executive leadership, six sigma black belt/champion process certified, Certified Change Specialist, Licensed Health/Life Insurance Advisor and over twenty years of Fortune 100 Corporate leadership growing from startups to Global Billion Dollar businesses. After all that GOD had a greater purpose and intention for her life. Suddenly life hit and she was flattened on her back with no corporate career and uncertain physical/mental capabilities after a postpartum stroke and brain hemorrhage with two toddlers at home. Later to start a foundation to help others called; I Believe Organization. This began a new entrepreneurial journey started with much uncertainty in parallel. All this only to fill Gods goal for her life. Now she is on a mission to bless even more people as an author/speaker! Her two boys Logan and Myles are the joys of my life! Her life motto now is "Maximizing Moments"!

Connection Info:

Email: Candice@Acethestrategy.com

Website: www.Acethestrategy.com

LinkedIn: www.linkedin.com/in/candice-nicholson-gaddy

~ Chapter 7 ~

Tammy Williams

Rocky Roads Are Beautiful

When I hear the words Rocky Road many things come to mind like challenges, being. Unbalanced, hard times, opportunities without a roadmap of success but mostly desserts that are a little crunchy/hard, delicious, and sweet at the same time. Interesting because it sounds a lot like life, doesn't it? I don't think any not of us are exempt from the rocky roads in life. Its how we will get through them. For arguments sake with no judgment, we can probably agree that each of our interpretation of a rocky road is different. Whatever the situation we need to be mindful to others and their situations they call a rocky road even when we fill it is just be a bump in the road. A Pastor once said if Gods going to bring you to it, he will bring you through it!

Inner peace is one of my favorite topics because I truly believe that not everything can be achieved without it. Lack of inner peace doe does not mean we are broken, but the benefit of having inner peace is as good as having it all and it shows up. We all know them, the people that have gone through or are going through major bad life situations but do not wear it and know one would even know because they keep showing up. I believe we all have an inner muscle which is a gage to our inner peace even if we do not know it. I think it is extremely important not to blame ourselves

SELF IMPOERMENT RESET

for every rocky road in life because we know that sometimes the rocky roads in life can be caused by others and this is why we need to utilize the inner peace muscle.

I was focusing so much on my adulthood, but to go back to my younger self if there were any situations that attempted to rob me of knowing and experiencing inner peace. I like to call it pealing an onion to really find out what may have impacted me negatively. As a young person, I had no idea what inner peace was. To move forward I literally had to take inventory of some my life experiences to see what had not been addressed and how they impacted to in a not so positive way. What I do know is that for me, inner peace comes in the form of letting it GO like a worn-out damaged pair of shoes — cleaning house per say. It can start from as little as creating boundaries and not letting others have a negative impact on our emotions. Finding the things that feed ones soul makes all the difference in the world.

I am thrilled to say that I have found some things that feed my soul: daily positive affirmations — because our ears are listening and reading! It is like a mini vacation; I also find colouring very relaxing and improves mood. I find positive relationships also help with the feeling of happiness. I also find going to the lake which also drowns out the negative noise and voices. Taking care of indoor and outdoor plants, appreciating nature, not feeling resentful towards others, (it is calming,) and training my mind not to care about everything along the way. With not using precious time to understand everything, it is empowering -and not STUFF!

As a child growing up, I was raised to love my neighbors and to think of others before myself. My beautiful rocky road did not show up until Junior High public school pre-

SELF IMPOERMENT RESET

teen age. I remember The Junior high school Tammy sitting in English class receiving a note from the teacher to bring home a report card with the words of recommendation that I should be removed from Advanced English and should be transferred to General English because my aptitude was not good enough to be in Advanced English. This hit me hard. I had never had challenges in any subject before. I experienced a mix bag of emotions; sadness, second guessing myself, my confidence was shattered, embarrassment because I had move to a different classroom and be separated from my many childhood friends whom I had known for years from early on at this very impressionable age where I was just beginning to get my footing into being molded into a bright young woman. The many pointed questions directed at me, not anyone else, some of my classmates noticing and saying: "wow that teacher is always picking on you." To not making the junior girls basketball team and my friends that did make the team — being more shocked than I was.

From being invited to several friends, homes for the first time and not being allowed to return based on their parents. Being questioned by some wanting to know where I was born. This is the part of my young life where I did not know where I belonged, and I literally became somewhat of a chameleon. I did not share this with anyone not even my mom. Thankfully, I had some family, friends, a loving church family plus my beautiful strong mother who was a pregnant widow at a young age that had demonstrated her resilience and exuded confidence while she raised three children. God bless her and God blessed me for having her as my mom.

It was not until my last years of high school when we moved to Toronto the metropolitan city where things really

SELF IMPOERMENT RESET

changed for the good me. I was able to restore my confidence. This Rocky Road as some may have called it was being paved to a proper, even flexible, light igniting, stylish, scenic, a little bumpy but beautiful path for my journey. I chose not to live in the past. As a young person I did not let the rocky road I endured be the reason for me not to attempt to do more or be more. Giving ourselves permission to feel the way we for just minute will help us build on our inner peace.

Writing a short note can be very therapeutic to having inner peace and bring closure. Here is a letter I wrote in my journal to help me gain inner peace.

Dear Teacher/Coach:

Thank you for helping to shape me and being part of the fuel that ignited in my drive. You may be surprised to know that upon moving to Toronto I was the Captain of the Junior Basketball Team, I was the MVP for many College Basketball Tournaments, I was the Female Athlete of the week for All the Ontario Colleges I worked many years in the publishing space as an Associate Publisher, Sales/Marketing role where I trained others and created compelling emails and email marketing campaigns. Some of the many lessons I have learnt:

But GOD

Be You

Never Quit

Love Others

Love Yourself

Self care is not selfish!

SELF IMPOERMENT RESET

The right attitude will take you places you desire. Having inner peace is a big missing link to success in life. Success is different to everyone from personal/business relationships, health, happiness, servant leadership, time freedom, I do not believe we can be happy or our best self without it.

There is so much power in finding inner peace. It has led me to more happiness, clarity, calm stress levels, better decision making, helps to alleviate fears in this beautiful chaotic world when things are going wrong. Just like Grandmas Rocky Road recipe that we require all of the ingredients for optimal taste we need to find our rocky road to inner peace recipe for optimal empowerment.

SELF IMPOERMENT RESET

~ Tammy Williams ~

Tammy Williams is a 5x International Best-Selling Author with over Fifteen years in marketing and sales. She is a collaboration and sales/marketing leader that is great at providing solutions for clients. From existing businesses to the brick and transitioning to click an order. She helps clients monetize on their websites with various social media strategies and marketing campaigns. She is also a Business Mentor to graduating business students of Access Employment and is a proud member of MP Resilient Women International Women Group. Advisory Board Member for Camera's for Girl's a registered Charity.

The Founder of Women, Champagne, and Real Estate and CryptoSmart Chicks. The goal is to empower women with all things real estate and crypto. She believes we all can give, and she started a Walk a Mile in her shoes campaign several years ago and has been able to collect over 400 pairs of ladies new and gently worn footwear which has been donated to various places in Durham region.

Home - Women Champagne and Real Estate

https://womenchampagneandrealestate.com/blogs/
She can be found on social media:

Facebook Women, Champagne and Realestate

https://www.facebook.com/groups/womenchampagnerealestate/?ref=share

~ Chapter 8 ~

Karen Hewitt

Go Ahead and Look in The Mirror

Go ahead and look in the mirror! Seriously, take a minute and look at yourself. I want you to pay attention. What color are your eyes? Your hair? Are you smiling? Now look deeper, who do you see? For me, it used to be a list of titles; even in the last several years, I added more. Yet it wasn't me. I didn't see me. Today when I look in the mirror, the perspective that I see now versus what I used to see, even though they have some elements of the same, is very different. This is how I know I have made my way through the journey of inner peace.

The hardest part of the journey is realizing that it is not this quick fix or a magic wand. We wake up and say: "Hey, I want inner peace, I want joy, I want happiness." and somehow, we expect them just to happen because we said so. I can remember as a teen being miserable and hiding huge portions of who I was because of bullying, then enduring an abusive marriage. Still looking in that mirror and seeking that peace. Every day, getting annoyed at the fact that I woke up and was miserable still.

A decade ago, I realized that if I wanted that to change, then the change had to start with me, and it's what began my personal development journey. Honestly, I was very reluctant to begin. I would pick up the book, roll my eyes,

SELF IMPOERMENT RESET

and read. I would watch the video, I then hired a coach and started going to networking events. Each day I would still look in that mirror and list out what I could see. It started as sad, lonely, ugly, afraid, criticizing every molecule of myself, trapped, hurting. These words kept repeating daily.

The next step was to start writing these observations down, so that's what I did, yet I didn't like them, so I started asking questions: why did I feel this way? Who told me to feel this way? Each day, my entries got longer as I questioned the reasoning behind each of these negative thoughts. As I questioned them, I broke down the barriers that held me back. There were really dark moments, and there were days when I didn't see how this could come out in a good light. My psyche was in a place due to so many traumas, fears, and self-hatred that not working on these for years tied me up so tight that I never thought it would end. To share how dark it was, there were days when I didn't want to wake up. I never wanted to do anything to take it into my own hands, but maybe, just maybe, if was time, it would be ok. I didn't go to Dr.'s appointments; I did not seek any help with my health, and I never tried to make new friends. I allowed my world to get smaller and smaller.

I had the trauma of having a serial killer for a doctor, bullies, emotional abuse, physical abuse, and an ex-husband who tried to unalive me, I had religious trauma from being in a religion that told me that without children I was worthless. That I was a bad person. I had the trauma of not allowing myself to live freely because of judgment. In the last seven years, I added a medically complex child that I had to fight for every step of the way.

SELF IMPOERMENT RESET

Almost lost him to drowning in 2020; I pulled him out of the pool, gave CPR, and he is still with us, and he is happy. I also had the challenges of living undiagnosed with ADHD and autism, which I only found out about in 2022 and 2023. I craved inner peace, but my internal world was in turmoil. It started to change in 2016. I hit rock bottom; my mum passed away with only a day's warning. She went to the hospital with stomach pain, and within 5 days of walking into that door, we found she had cancer that was untreatable; she must have been in so much pain that it was impossible to understand. Then she was gone. my best friend in the entire world was gone. My only piece of peace left. She had encouraged me to write down, to ask questions, and told me how I didn't need to hold her on a pedestal and that she held me there because I endured so much without sharing it with her, she asked me to not hold it in. She started my journey. When she was gone, I shut down and retreated into a world where no one could reach me. I stopped talking to friends, stopped interacting with people. I couldn't even go to her funeral because it was in the UK. I didn't have my passport, and I had a newborn that relied on me. It took several months, and I picked up the pen again and started looking in the mirror.

The words my mum spoke resonated: "You survived because someone else might not. have, tell that story." With out realizing it, I started to write more positive statements. Many of which I recognize what my mum had said. I started to see myself as this individual without the titles. Strong, resilient, smart, logical, big-picture thinker, compassionate, empathic, Loving, Listener, Heart, Hope. Each of these words became a stepping stone on my road to inner peace. I built on them, asking the questions the same way I did with the negative words I spoke to myself. I started to take mini actions. The first step was to leave the

SELF IMPOERMENT RESET

house, something I hadn't done unless it was a baby/child/pregnancy appointment in years. I started networking and learning to speak my story, first, was all about overcoming the domestic violence I had endured, and then it was about sharing being brave and authentic on social media, where I helped small business owners grow and excel. As well as helping the team members in network marketing.

Each word I wanted to understand and feel, see how it related to me in a way that impacted not only me but my kids as well. When the pandemic hit, I realized how I had started to need the connection I had developed beforehand and started to slide back into darkness. It also became a time when I asked myself more core questions about who I was, instead of crying at the answers, I saw hope and light. I added meditation and the first time I meditated; I fell asleep, same on the second, third, and probably up to the fiftieth. I also found myself asking why I was doing this, and my mind wandered, but then I got comfortable with the sound of my voice in my mind. Realizing that I could sit calmly and quietly with myself. This was a great step to that inner peace. However, when I realized that I had finally made it was 2022. I took several large steps. I left the religion officially and legally, which had traumatized me. I stopped playing the dutiful doormat wife that I only played because of past abuse and religious expectations. Began to focus on my happiness and that of my kids. I also came out as queer, something I had shoved down deep inside because of hateful comments and expectations of what a woman needed to be. I was not afraid anymore. I received comments about how I needed to be saved, how this made me a bad person.

SELF IMPOERMENT RESET

Instead of going back into the shadows, I had the inner peace to stand for who I am. I started to take my medical seriously and found out I was neuro-spicy, and some people who knew me, weren't surprised at all. I also found out about the autoimmune challenges I had and started treating them. Something that my dark shadows prevented me from doing before. I forgave but didn't forget my ex-husband, who tried to beat me to death. All these shadowy ropes that had bound me with negativity were fraying and not holding me back anymore. I had to do the work to find that moment, had to sit with the emotions, the thoughts, and pain.

How I knew I had finally found my inner peace was when I looked in that mirror and said with no caveats. "I see me." "Do you see you or do you see the lists?" "I see me." Do you see you? Or do you see the lists?

SELF IMPOERMENT RESET

~ Karen Hewitt ~

Empowering Connections, Building Relationships

Karen Hewitt, born in England and now living in the USA, is a top social media strategist and network marketer. A mom of five, she balances family and career with ease and a healthy dose of sarcasm. As a member of the LGBTQIA community and a neurodiverse individual, Karen brings a unique perspective to her work.

With a loving and compassionate nature, she fosters authentic connections and builds strong relationships. Karen advocates against discrimination and hate, believing in kindness and respect for all. She creates a supportive, inclusive community through her expertise, helping others achieve their goals in social media and network marketing.

Links

www.BlossomToSuccess.com

https://www.facebook.com/blossomtosuccess

https://www.instagram.com/blossomtosuccess/

~ Chapter 9 ~
~ Julz Vitality ~
From Ashes to Light

Let's pause for a moment…Let's ask ourselves a few questions of reflection. Am I happy today? Do I have a generally happy life, or perhaps I struggle through it, and it seems like a rocky road with many unexpected turns? Do I strive for or desire a better future, perhaps, a more peaceful and fulfilling one? Do I wonder what's missing, and how come others seem to have seemingly happier lives?

I contemplate these questions from time to time. They move me to dig for the answers. Over a period of several years, I have found some concepts that shed a different perspective on life, happiness, and peace. You may have heard others recommending "taking control" of your live, while others say, "go with the flow, don't force it," yet others say, "design a desired outcome." These approaches seem to be contradictory at first glance. Let's explore them and a few related ones through an illustration of my story, which, although unique, is also typical to many. Let's see if you can draw some parallels with your life, and let's see if we have more in common than you may think. Right now, I'm a stranger to you. I hope to change that by the end of this chapter. My goal is to empower you to dream bigger, live more peacefully, and be content with each moment, while still cherishing a dream in your mind's eye.

SELF IMPOERMENT RESET

My story begins in the SU, a land where individuality was discouraged, and conformity was the norm. Everything was uniform, from the school clothes to everyone wearing 1 brand of clothing since foreign manufacturers were not allowed in the country. Individuality was choked out for the sake of the spirit of the community and the collective. Social and communication skills were neglected, and success in academics was blown out of proportion. I was taught to be a 'gray mouse,' to blend in and avoid drawing attention to myself. We had no choice but to suppress our emotions, opinions and extraordinary talents or interests. Obedience and loyalty to the rules and the authorities was rewarded, while any attempt to express individuality in any way, shape or form was looked down on, if not punished.

At nineteen years old, everything changed when my family migrated to Canada. My father delusionally craved the stability that differences in past societal structures once provided him and imagined that Canada would return the structure of those former past societal structures. Once republics started separating and gaining independence, 'Perestroika' (the rebuilding) came with a lot of chaos, introducing capitalistic elements and freedoms foreign to my father. So, he made a risky jump, to a country he knew almost nothing about, the language he didn't speak, and the new life he imagined would solve all our problems. Although Canada did offer some social benefits, healthcare, free language classes for newcomers, and even a community of ex-sovies to associate with, my dad was completely lost in the economy, completely ignorant of concepts like credit, interest, real estate, and ownership of any kind. He and my mom lived in the same rental high-rise for twenty-five-years while they could have paid off a mortgage —another concept he never fully fathomed.

SELF IMPOERMENT RESET

How about us kids? I was nineteen and my brother twelve. Although the language shock was really tough, despite my prior preparation for arrival, I didn't understand a word of the Canadian spoken English. In school we were taught by the British kind. Learning to move around the city, taking public transit to our English school, and even buying groceries, were activities that tested us beyond what we ever knew how to do in a western world. If you immigrated, or even travelled to a foreign land, you can imagine the struggle such simple activities can create, and the effect they had on our family.

Nevertheless, bit by bit, we started to get accustomed. For the first time, I tasted freedom—the freedom to speak my mind, to pursue my dreams, and to live life on my terms. I was the pioneer among my family and community, hungry to learn new ways, and understand new concepts. I figured out the concept of bank accounts, credit cards, credit lines and loans. I took driver training, got a licence, then a car, a cell phone…remember those Motorola flip phones? I fulfilled my dream of getting a gym membership, although it was embarrassing as I now look back at it… I showed up in the gym in Jane Fonda aerobics attire, wondering why people were staring at me. I realized "English as a second language" class was doing nothing for me and signed myself up for 'high school for adults,' where native dropouts had a chance to get their diplomas. That was like an ice bucket over my head. No one cared that I was an immigrant. Do the work or fail. I had struggled through the first few weeks wanting to quit from embarrassment and inability to even follow instructions given by a native instructor who cared less about my situation. I gave a presentation in one of the classes about Theory of Evolution and kept saying SPICES instead of species. The class was making fun of me throughout this

SELF IMPOERMENT RESET

already embarrassing 'public speaking' performance. I stuck through it, and in a matter of a semester, I was an almost fluent English speaker, way surpassing my community, family, and even classmates with my hard-earned As and A+s. It gave me the confidence that I CAN get through tough times, and those times are actually the ones that help you grow and improve the most!

The Western world offers us freedoms of choice and lifestyle, ability to dream and explore options. However, its governmental systems and social programming lead most of us, as an obedient flock, to what I call, the MATRIX. You would do well in life if and only if you follow the beaten path of post-secondary education, a stable corporate career, and the pursuit of conventional success, climbing the ladder, getting a house with a two-car garage, a shed at the back to store your lawnmower, and your two-week vacation and a 2% raise a year (numbers may vary). It ropes us into another type of slavery, while offering the freedom of a capitalist lifestyle, security of a home and a place to raise a family. Many fall into that trap, partially because it's marketed so well, and everywhere. I did too…

For two decades, I thrived in the corporate world as a business analyst, manager, and project consultant. I discovered and refined many of my technical skills, and even learnt a lot about sales, marketing, and communication on my own accord after work. I now bought and sold several houses, owned many nice cars, was in my second marriage, had my two kids, living the 'dream' in a prestigious neighborhood, socializing with 'good' friends, pursuing hobbies, growing a garden, and really… had anything for I wanted. Having jumped from corporate employers, climbing the ladder, becoming a consultant, a manager, a VP, making over $120K a year, having a full

SELF IMPOERMENT RESET

benefits package and four weeks of vacation — I could not seem to desire more!

Something did not make sense though. I was living the dream defined. A slave to someone else's dream to make ends meet, owning a house with a mortgage, two cars, and all the expenses to maintain those, I needed to work long hours and far from home. Waking up before dawn, driving to a train station to catch a train at 6:15 am to be at work by 7:30 was a norm. Getting home at 6:30 pm after dark, grabbing a few groceries on my way, cooking dinner and making lunches for everyone, just to crash into bed at midnight exhausted, and repeat it all over again the next day… This turned into an inevitable race of life, the norm I was starting to gradually resent. Work gave me a sense of accomplishment, but was it fulfilling? Being important and competent felt good, but was I making a difference? Would anyone remember me when I'm no longer there? Beneath the surface, a cognitive dissonance was brewing. The life I was living did not align with my true self, and a burnout was in the brew.

The universe had a plan, it seems. Since I refused to wake up when pressure was applied, more pressure was needed. Life threw a few more curveballs at me, and not long after my world the way I knew it was suddenly shattered in pieces. A violent incident between my father and my husband at the time, followed by an infidelity discovered 9 months later, and a few more tragic events I don't want to delve into, were enough to make me question everything I knew about life. I was left hanging off a cliff, teetering on the edge of despair, and plunged into a mental health crisis.

Months of darkness followed, but deep within me, a phoenix stirred. This resilient part of me decided that I had suffered enough. I remember the morning I dragged myself

SELF IMPOERMENT RESET

out of bed thinking "I am sick of being sick, depressed, and tired. Something has to change. Universe, show me a way out!" Little by little I began to climb out of the abyss, grasping at every straw of hope I could find — whether it was physical, emotional, or spiritual healing. It was not easy, but slowly, I rebuilt myself. And from the ruins of my old life, I birthed a new one. My business emerged, using the ashes of my past to fertilize the blossoming movement of Positive Impact Media.

With tens of thousands of dollars invested and years of relentless learning, I've become a champion for those who seek a life of freedom, joy, and purpose. I now run a boutique visibility firm that creates stages for impact-makers and supports them with marketing and visibility strategies. As a podcaster, show host, and publisher of Positive Impact Media, my mission is to empower conscious entrepreneurs to design a business they love and a life of which they are proud to live.

I am grateful for all my coaches, and every single guest on my show or an author published in our Positive Impact Magazine, because each of their stories healed me and equipped me to be stronger. I hope you join the tripe of impact makers and say hello, since I would love to meet you, and get to know you!

Do you feel like your story can heal someone? I invite you to join forces with VitalityVirtual.org, a non-for-profit virtual wellness platform to spread healing to those who need it the most, those who, like me, are sick and tired of being sick and are looking for a lifesaver. Our partners conduct virtual live classes (like those fitness classes in the gym), create transformation and empower those who reached out for help and made a decision to grow, improve and reach alignment. Our collaborations with other non-

SELF IMPOERMENT RESET

profit organizations are reinforcing our mission to spread healing to those who raised their hand to ask for help, as well as segments of the global population where healing, mental health and personal growth are less acceptable or not so accessible.

Are you passionate about creating a legacy, healing others, or helping those who are on the journey of self improvement? I invite you to join the Positive Impact Circle, our Facebook Community, where you can connect with like-minded visionaries and participate in regular networking events. Together, we can step into the spotlight and embrace the glory that we all deserve. Let's create a world where freedom, joy, and purpose are the norm, not the exception. What helps me to maintain peace and vitality on a day-to-day basis today? Here are my top tips as a gift to you, my dear reader **https://1.pitv.ca/3tips**.

One final thought. I hope you can see how in the midst of a crisis, we seem to feel stuck and not know the way out. Faith, and trust that everything will work out at the end, is what helps us persevere, even with no visible improvement. Just like going to the gym for a month because we are on a mission, offering consistent committed action. Results and improvement are inevitable. Stay the course, keep your dream in mind, and join communities of positive individuals, read, and watch uplifting information, and take care of the best gift you have - your body and your mind. All setbacks are temporary, and there is always a rainbow after the storm.

SELF IMPOERMENT RESET

~ Julz Vitality ~

Julz Vitality is a wellness & mental health advocate, publicist, show host, and a business mentor. She runs a non-profit virtual platform for mindset experts and healers gifted in energetic and alternative modalities. Get to know her and get in touch: via http://VitalityVirtual.org where you can also find all our platforms and socials.

Website & Socials:

http://prjulz.com - Gifts, Resources, Calendar, Social Icons, Events

3 Hacks to Greater Peace & Vitality:
https://1.pitv.ca/3tips

~ Chapter 10 ~

Michelle Lee

The Rocky Road Brings You Success

Have you ever felt like you were doing everything you could to survive the rollercoaster of life, but everything was crumbling around you? Life can sometimes feel like not just a rocky road but a road that is headed right off a cliff with no escape!

From as early as I can remember, this was my life. It just seemed like the harder I tried, the worse it got. Everything seemed like a fight, and I was losing that fight! You see, as a child, I lived in a home with a narcissistic father who controlled everything. My mom and my brother were easy targets for my dad. For example, my mom was never allowed to get her drivers license, so she was completely dependent on my dad for everything, and my brother is legally blind. I, on the other hand, didn't want that and fought him with every ounce I had. My goal was to break every rule and stand up for all of us.

I spent the majority of my childhood and teen years fighting with that man and doing everything I could NOT to be like him. When I was younger, he sometimes worked from home and my mom would have to try to keep us entertained so we didn't make any noise at all when he

SELF IMPOERMENT RESET

was on his calls for work. He would mentally beat us up daily and I would get so angry at my mom for not standing up for herself.

I started running away at a very young age, but he always seemed to find me and bring me back to my hell! I officially left at 18! I couldn't believe I was finally free!! So, I thought, I gave up going to college to have my freedom and finally try to live a normal life. I had no idea what normal was, but I was sure I could find it.

It's funny how sometimes you have to keep repeating and making the same mistakes beating your head against the wall. Then you learn the hard way. This makes you become the person you need to be. Repeating the mistakes when I thought I was free. My father sucked me back into his world by offering me a job, and well, I was broke and was going from one dead-end job to another. I succumbed to the pressure and ended up working for him for years. That story is a book unto itself.

As for my personal life, I ended up getting married not once but twice. Both of these men were just like my father. I now realized it was filled with nothing but mental abuse and chaos. For example, I remember once being in a car with my ex-husband; I did something that made him angry, so he shut the headlights off on a dark country road, nailed the gas, and he drove as fast as he could and wouldn't stop until I was crying, and screaming so much that he slammed on the breaks and told me to get out. It ended shortly after that, and to top it off, he slept with my best friend.

SELF IMPOERMENT RESET

The second marriage lasted much longer because I had built up a really thick skin at this point, I was numb. We were married for about ten years and brought me two beautiful children. However, this relationship was worse than the first. I would do it all again to have my two incredible children.

Has anyone ever said to you everything happens for a reason? When someone said those words to me, I would get so angry! I never believe it. Until one day, someone introduced me to the personal development world. I had no idea what personal development even was. It was exactly what I needed.

My belief is life is a journey and God has a plan! You have to believe! I had many lessons to learn in life, I am still learning every day. Every bump in the road, every sinkhole I fell into was God telling me I needed to learn a lesson or make a change to grow into the person I needed to be. I realized that everything does happen for a reason. Looking back on my life now, I can connect the dots. I had to go through it all to become the person I am. I needed to find my purpose and live the life God put me on this earth for, my love for people. Every single moment has to happen, the good, the bad, and everything in between, for you to grow.

Every moment grew me as a person and gave me the strength, and the ability to grow my faith. I am now living my best life with the man of my dreams. I have two beautiful kids, two amazing bonus kids, and two incredible grand- babies, oh, and I can't forget our crazy fur baby, Harley.

SELF IMPOERMENT RESET

In my personal development journey, I learned the secret to understanding yourself and others, now I am helping others to become the best version of themselves. Let your pain be your purpose. God has a plan, once you embrace the journey and put your trust in Him things will change. Keep believing that the rocky road can bring you success and you will become the light the world needs.

SELF IMPOERMENT RESET

~ Michelle Lee ~

Michelle Lee is an award-winning Certified BANK Coach and Licensed Trainer, Keynote Speaker, and Networking Ninja. She has more than 30 years of experience in Corporate Sales and many years in Network Marketing and Direct Sales. Implementing BANK, she took her start-up company from 0 to over $2 million in less than three years, BANK saved her relationship with her son. Seeing the power of BANK, Michelle knew she had found her purpose and passion. Her mission is to empower the lives of every person she touches and have a ripple effect so others can learn to live their best life ever, having financial and time freedom and the best relationships possible.

https://www.linkedin.com/in/michelle-myrter/

https://www.facebook.com/myrter

https://www.instagram.com/michellelee_721/

SELF IMPOERMENT RESET

~ Chapter 11 ~
Cedric Singleton
From Soldier to Salesman

In 1993, I was a young Army officer stationed at Fort Carson in Colorado Springs. My life seemed to be set in stone—I was freshly married, with a 12-year-old bonus son, and a baby on the way. My future appeared clear and predictable, or so I thought. I had a plan: a long, prosperous military career—a steady path that I had always envisioned. Then one evening, everything changed. It all began with a junior military officers corporate recruitment conference at Fort Carson. Several medical companies were looking for disciplined, detail-oriented officers to become sales professionals for their businesses. A few buddies and I decided to attend. I'll never forget the energy in the room.

As the recruiters spoke, something inside me clicked. The idea of selling medical solutions to healthcare organizations felt like a new frontier—a world that combined problem-solving, strategy, and high-stakes responsibility that I thrived on. The more I listened, the more I realized that this could be an incredible opportunity to grow both professionally and personally. I began interviewing with top medical companies, and soon, I received an offer from Abbott Laboratories to take on a sales territory in South Texas. Let me paint the picture again: I was a young officer in the Army, with a pregnant

SELF IMPOERMENT RESET

wife, a 12-year-old son who would be leaving his friends and everything familiar, and a military career that was supposed to define my future. Now, I was facing the decision to leave it all behind—leaving the security and structure of military life for the uncertainty of a civilian career in sales.

It felt like jumping off a cliff, with no guarantee that I'd land on my feet. I had to assure my family that I knew what I was doing. The pressure was immense. I was about to leave behind everything I had worked for, stepping away from the military's comfort and discipline, and embracing an uncertain future in sales. The responsibility was overwhelming. How could I convince my wife and son that this was the right move? How could I leave the certainty of the Army for a career in an industry I knew little about?

I had no choice but to stretch. Just like a rubber band that pulls tight, the only way I would grow was if I embraced the tension—the pressure that came with stepping outside my comfort zone. Growth doesn't happen when you stay where it's safe. It happens when you're forced to stretch, to move past the limits of what you know. It happens when the tension between who you are and who you could be pushes you to evolve. And that's exactly what I had to do—leave the safety of the military, to dive headfirst into a new chapter that would test me in ways I never imagined. But that challenge was the key to my growth, and there was no turning back. As a result, I had a very successful thirty-year career in corporate America. There was lots of growth and stretching along the way!

SELF IMPOERMENT RESET

From Charleston to the DMV: A Brave New World

My roots trace back to Charleston, South Carolina—fondly known as Chucktown by those with a bit of swag. Growing up there, I had a solid childhood. The sense of community was strong, blending the slow pace of the country with the bustle of city life, and always surrounded by family. My sister, Trice, my cousins, and I were inseparable. We did everything together. And as for school? I excelled—honor roll, good grades, and an abundance of friends. But when I was twelve, everything changed. My parents divorced, and my mom, seeking new opportunities, enlisted in the Army. We were soon stationed at Walter Reed in the Washington, DC area, and we had to leave behind everything that was familiar.

Moving to Maryland (outside of DC) was an enormous adjustment. The new environment, the different people, and the academic challenges were unlike anything I had experienced before. My world in Charleston had been stable and predictable, but here, everything felt foreign. The school system was more demanding, and I had trouble keeping up. On top of that, I carried a strong Geechee-Gullah accent from Charleston, and the other kids made fun of me for it. At first, I felt completely out of place, and I couldn't shake the feeling of insecurity that crept in.

I still remember telling my mom I wanted to go back to Charleston. School was tough, the kids weren't very welcoming, and I didn't feel like I belonged. But my mom, with a steady gaze, looked me in the eyes and said something that has stuck with me ever since. I know this is hard for you right now, but I've never known you to be a quitter. Her words hit me like a ton of bricks. It wasn't just encouragement—it was a challenge.; I've never known you to be a quitter. Those words became a turning point. I

SELF IMPOERMENT RESET

stopped wallowing in self-pity and started pushing myself. I dedicated hours to catching up with the curriculum, and despite my Charleston accent, I began raising my hand in class—asking and answering questions. I wasn't going to be a quitter. Slowly, but surely, my grades improved, and my confidence returned. By the time I reached high school, I was back to my old self—even stronger. I had learned the value of persistence and hard work in the face of adversity.

Life Lessons from My Experiences

The struggles I faced as a young kid in Maryland were uncomfortable, no doubt, but they also became some of the most important lessons of my life. The pain of being different, of struggling to fit in, and of battling insecurities shaped me in ways I could never have anticipated. That period of adjustment taught me discipline, structure, and resilience—the very qualities that would carry me through the challenges of military life, corporate America, and eventually, entrepreneurship.

What I learned during those formative years is that growth isn't always easy. It doesn't happen when you're comfortable or when everything is going well. Growth happens when you are pushed beyond your limits, when you're faced with adversity that forces you to stretch. In the military, I had already learned how to push myself physically and mentally, but that moment of deciding to step into the unknown world of sales brought a new kind of challenge—a personal and professional one that required me to grow in entirely different ways.

In both cases, there is a very important point - Growth doesn't just happen. It requires intentional effort. It requires you to push through the fear and discomfort. It requires you to be stretched to your limits. And it is

SELF IMPOERMENT RESET

through those moments of tension that we discover just how much we are truly capable of. The key to growth isn't avoiding the hard stuff—it's embracing it. It's accepting that growth is a process—a continuous journey of learning, stretching, and evolving. Embrace the discomfort. It's where growth begins.

SELF IMPOERMENT RESET

~ Cedric Singleton ~

Cedric began his professional journey as an officer in the U.S. Army before launching a corporate career that would span three decades. Upon leaving the military, he joined Abbott Laboratories, where he dedicated 27 years to various sales and marketing roles, including:

- Sales Executive
- Advertising Product Manager
- Regional Sales Director
- Global Director of Sales Operations

Throughout his tenure at Abbott, Cedric and his teams consistently earned recognition for high performance and commercial excellence. This success led to his recruitment by Carrier Global, where he was tasked with building and leading a new commercial Revenue Operations department as its Global Director. Under his leadership, the team achieved double-digit revenue growth, raising annual revenue from $615 million to $1.2 billion in just three years. Now retired from his corporate career, Cedric is the founder and owner of Peak Performance Leadership Institute. He is a corporate speaker and leadership coach, where his focus is to help individuals and organizations achieve their Peak Performance by Mastering Fundamentals. In addition, Peak Performance Leadership Institute helps small businesses achieve the same financial success as large corporations like Abbott and Carrier.

SELF IMPOERMENT RESET

Cedric holds a BA in Political Science from Howard University and an MBA from the University of Memphis. He is certified as a Trainer, Coach, and Speaker with The John Maxwell Team and Corporate Training Executive. In his community, Cedric serves as the Director of Education and Vice President of the Alpha Foundation with his fraternity, Alpha Phi Alpha, Inc. He is also the Co-Chair of the Business and Education Committee for the Charles County Chamber of Commerce. Cedric has been married to Dee Dee for 31 years, and together they have three wonderful children.

Founder and Owner: Peak Performance Leadership Institute

Website: www.thepeakleadership.com

FB: cedricsingleton1906

IG: cedricsingleton1906

LinkedIn: www.linkedin.com/in/cedricsingleton

~ Chapter 12 ~

Julia Flynn Werre

A Dream Life Built from Hardship

Today, I'm living a life that feels like the end of a rom-com—Prince Charming, a dream job, endless travel, and a backyard full of cats who think I'm their queen. But let's not kid ourselves; getting here wasn't a montage of inspirational music and feel-good moments. It was years of crawling through the trenches with heartbreak, self-doubt, and that nagging voice whispering, "What if you fail?"

But then I remembered the words from Peter Pan: "But, oh my darling, what if you fly?" So, I kept going. Every stumble taught me resilience, and every heartbreak led me closer to the life I was meant to live.

Manifesting Prince Charming

Learning from the Past

Two failed marriages taught me:

Don't settle for crumbs when you deserve a feast.

Integrity isn't negotiable.

SELF IMPOERMENT RESET

Love isn't about saving someone or being saved; it's about partnership.

Manifesting Love

Armed with The Rules and He's Just Not That into You, I got clear on what I wanted. I wrote a list: kindness, humor, honesty, and a deep love for who I am. Then I stuck to my boundaries like my life depended on it.

The Reward

As Zig Ziglar said, "You don't have to be great to start, but you have to start to be great." And start I did. Prince Charming wasn't a magical rescue but a partner who met me exactly where I was. Together, we've built a relationship on trust, laughter, and a shared love for the chaos of everyday life.

The Infertility Battle

Round One: Alone and Heartbroken

At nineteen, I faced infertility with my first husband. I endured a painful hysterosalpingogram (HSG) alone, only for him to refuse to provide a sperm sample and tell me he wanted to separate. That heartbreak stayed with me, shaping how I approached future challenges.

Round Two: Together and Stronger

When I married Prince Charming, infertility treatments were a team effort. We went through: Endless tests and ultrasounds—three times a week for months on end. Multiple rounds of IUI and IVF—a rollercoaster of hope and heartbreak. A shared commitment—he held my hand through every injection, every failure, and every glimmer of hope.

SELF IMPOERMENT RESET

Even though the treatments didn't bring us a child, they brought us closer than ever. As Harriet Tubman said, "Every great dream begins with a dreamer." We dreamed together, and though the outcome wasn't what we planned, the journey strengthened our love.

Career Reinvention: From Chaos to Creativity

The Rollercoaster Years

Straight commission sales is not for the faint of heart—it's like professional gambling, but with better outfits. The highs were exhilarating, but the lows made me question every career choice I'd ever made. 2008 Real Estate

Bubble and Beyond

Then came the 2008 real estate crash, followed by the rise of social media. Suddenly, the rules changed overnight: Sales calls turned into hashtags. Networking events became algorithms. I had to learn, adapt, and evolve at a dizzying pace.

Finding My Passion

As Zig Ziglar said, "Difficult roads often lead to beautiful destinations." Those challenges pushed me to build a career that feels authentic and fulfilling. Now, I spend my days immersed in creativity, designing graphics, and helping others find their voice in a noisy world.

The Furry Family That Found Me

A Disney Movie with Barking

If you'd told me I'd one day, be managing a household of four Shih Tzus and a colony of feral cats, I would've

SELF IMPOERMENT RESET

laughed. But here I am: The Shih Tzus—royalty on four legs, whose main goal is to trip me when I least expect it. The Feral Cats—what started as a couple of strays is now an empire of eleven, who think I'm their full-time caterer.

Lessons in Love These animals have taught me:

Patience—feeding cats is like hosting a dinner party for picky eaters.

Laughter—every day brings some ridiculous moment I couldn't make up if I tried. **Purpose**—showing up for them has brought unexpected joy to my life.

Living the Dream

Travel, Creativity, and Connection

If my younger self could see me now, she'd probably say, "Who are you, and how did this happen?" I'm living a life full of:

Global Adventures—Traveling with my husband has broadened my perspective in ways I never imagined.

Creative Joy—Graphic design feels less like work and more like play.

Connection—Speaking on international stages and helping others find their own resilience is a dream come true.

Finding Purpose After Pain

As Harriet Tubman reminded me, "Always remember, you have within you the strength, the patience, and the passion to reach for the stars." Helping others rebuild their confidence after heartbreak or loss has become my passion. I've been where they are, and I know the road back isn't easy—but it's worth every step.

SELF IMPOERMENT RESET

Closing Thoughts: The Life I Love

My life today isn't perfect, but it's mine. Every challenge—every heartbreak, career reinvention, and personal struggle—brought me closer to the joy I feel now. I wake up every day grateful for my husband, my creative work, and the chance to help others feel powerful and successful after tragedy.

As Peter Pan said, "But, oh my darling, what if you fly?" I took the leap, and I found a life that's better than I ever dreamed.

SELF IMPOERMENT RESET

~ Julia Flynn Werre ~

Julia Flynn Werre is a seasoned network marketing strategist and Corporate Director at APLGO, known for fostering team growth and business success through tailored training and results-driven strategies. Raised by parents who were network marketers and entrepreneurs, Julia was inspired from an early age to believe she could achieve anything. Her personal experiences with infertility and autoimmune disease also deeply influence her coaching, providing her with a unique perspective that resonates with clients. Combining expertise with empathy, Julia empowers entrepreneurs to unlock their potential and achieve sustainable growth.

Julia Flynn Werre | 410-978-8555 |
JuliaFlynnWerre.com

Calendar Link: http://time.healthydnacandy.com

~ Chapter 13 ~

Dr. Andrea Adams-Miller

Choosing The High Road: A Journey from Chaos to Conviction

In our lives, the arduous journey from chaos to conviction is more than a path; it's a profound transformation, sometimes never-ending, but when you finally reach your destination, there is a rebirth into self-empowerment and inner peace that you never believed could happen. This chapter is a glimpse of how I guide you through this transformative process, drawing from my expertise in neuroscience and strategic personal branding and my challenging path with twists and turns, obstacles, and roadblocks. Together, we navigate this terrain, turning turmoil into triumph and uncertainty into unwavering strength.

Cultivating a Groundwork of Understanding

Let's start with the brain—the command center of our emotions and behaviors. Neuroscience teaches us that each thought and response is a mere flicker in our minds subconscious. By understanding these flickers and how they merge to become stories that no longer serve us, we can begin to spin a new story for ourselves, one of empowerment and enlightened self-awareness. This understanding gives us the power to shape our thoughts and actions and instills a greater sense of control and

SELF IMPOERMENT RESET

confidence in us, leading to a more empowered and self-assured self. Imagine your mind as a garden. Each thought is a seed that can grow into a poisonous weed that chokes out the positive or a flourishing plant that bears fruit that feeds the soul. Mindfulness and reframing are tools—in the hands of people like me, like a gardener—that help you cultivate this landscape. I want to teach you to nurture your positive seeds and uproot the weeds of negativity. This cultivation must go beyond superficial; it's about altering the very soil of your thoughts to foster the growth you desire that aligns with your deepest values and aspirations before you are exposed to negativity.

Strategic Actions for Monumental Changes

Awareness is only the beginning. The real magic happens when you put that awareness into action. Think of yourself as a sculptor and your actions as the strokes that mold the shape of your human form. What kind of person will you sculpt? Will it reflect the true essence of your spirit and ambition? Strategic actions include setting specific goals, practicing self-reflection, engaging in activities that align with your values, aspirations, and hiring a mentor to help you mend your mind.

   Additionally, personal branding comes into play for individual life and business. It is much more than a marketing strategy; it is an expression of your unique identity. Personal branding involves crafting a public persona that resonates with your true self and paints a compelling world picture with authenticity where you get to be the real you. Each action you take and each decision you make should be deliberate and contribute to your modeling, which is this honest masterpiece of yours. It is about aligning your actions and behaviors with your values

SELF IMPOERMENT RESET

and goals, creating a consistent and authentic image of yourself, and feeling validated and genuine in the process.

Leveraging Knowledge as a Catalyst for Growth

Knowledge is your shield and your guide on this journey. While you might desire to dive into the latest advancements in neuroscience, such as understanding the brains plasticity and the role of neurotransmitters in mood regulation, to understand the and the why behind your behaviors and use this knowledge to steer your actions more effectively, you might find that working with a mentor like me that has already focused on the learning and forwarding the tools and tips to help you achieve your excellence with grace and ease so much simpler. Simultaneously, equip yourself with personal branding skills to navigate life's chaos intact and with flair. This dual approach—rooted in the solid science of the brain and the art of self-presentation—prepares you to face challenges with resilience and a pr but also a plan to thrive.

Blueprinting Your Future

Your personal blueprint—a detailed map of your journey from where you are to where you want to be—is the culmination of self-awareness, strategic action, and informed knowledge. This blueprint is more than a plan; it is a commitment to your future self, a contract you write with conviction and hope. This plan should detail your goals, the milestones you will encounter, and the strategies you will use to achieve them. Like any good architect, you must be prepared to reassess and adjust your blueprint as you gain more insights and experiences along your journey. You are the architect of your future, responsible for designing a path that aligns with your values and aspirations.

SELF IMPOERMENT RESET

Transforming Challenges into Opportunities

Every challenge you face on this journey is an opportunity to learn, grow, and excel. Growing up in a dysfunctional home, I struggled with people pleasing, taking on the responsibilities of others, and being an overachiever. While these were challenges, along the way, they allowed me to work positively in challenging situations, taking on celebrities, training overseas, and solving problems that seemingly could not be solved. You can turn the negative into positive yourself, so when faced with obstacles, use your newfound knowledge and strategies to navigate them. Along the way, seek help. While I had figured out how to be resilient much on my own, it was only after I invested in mentors to help me mold my mind, release the negative self-talk, and rewrite the stories to foster my strengths instead of focusing on my weaknesses that I overcame the biggest challenges of my life. Therefore, remember that the storms you endure can strengthen your roots and fortify your resolve. You can take the high road to protect yourself and make your dreams come true bigger than you ever desired.

Embracing the Power of Community

Focusing on what is most important. No journey should ever be a solo endeavor. While it is essential to have moments where you choose to be alone with yourself, along the way, continually seek out mentors, join positive professional communities, and surround yourself with supportive peers who share your future vision and values. These relationships are best served when they support you in who you want to be and where they challenge you positively to view your journey with new perspectives and insights that can enhance your growth.

SELF IMPOERMENT RESET

Celebrating Each Victory

Take time to celebrate your victories, no matter how small. If you said no for the first time, celebrate. If you stood your ground and asked for what you wanted, celebrate. Each success on your path is a testament to your courage and a building block for your future. These celebrations are more than acknowledging your progress; they fuel your motivation and remind you of the strength you possess deep within. Wins are a powerful tool to keep you moving forward on your journey, and they serve as a constant reminder of your progress and potential, keeping you motivated and acknowledged.

Conclusion: A Lifelong Journey of Growth

Your journey from chaos to conviction is a continuous learning, adapting, and evolving cycle. It is about becoming who you were meant to be and who you choose to be. When you finally know you can stand in the conviction of your ideas, thoughts, values, and opinions, you will be freer than you ever thought possible. Embrace each step with courage and confidence, knowing you can transform any turmoil into a testament to your strength with the right tools and mindset. I believe in you.

SELF IMPOERMENT RESET

~ Dr Andrea Adams-Miller ~

Dr. Andrea Adams-Miller, International Award-Winning Publicity Consultant and Master Neuroscientist is the CEO of The RED-Carpet Connection Publicity, Publishing, and Talent Agency. She harnesses her expert consulting strategies, robust mental performance toolkit, and $15 billion personal connections to turn the aspirations of elite entrepreneurs into a legacy.

As a global influencer, she has presented in 37 countries and made 3,500+ media appearances, including 20/20 and E! News. She has worked for celebrities like the Michael Jackson family, shared the stage with Sir Anthony Hopkins and Les Brown, and trained corporations like Sony and Google in Egypt and Dubai. Book a session with her and claim your free gift at www.TheREDCarpetConnection.com.

www.TheREDCarpetConnection.com.

SELF IMPOERMENT RESET

~Chapter 14 ~

Brendan McCauley

The Power of Starting Over: Lessons from My Rocky Road

Life is like a very stressful journey. Sometimes it's smooth and easy to sail, but other times, it feels rocky, difficult and never-ending. Along my journey, I've faced three major challenges that taught me the most valuable lessons about inner peace and resilience: losing weight as a kid, earning my MBA, and starting over after a long relationship ended. These challenges weren't easy, but they shaped who I am today. My hope is that by sharing my story can inspire you to keep pushing forward, no matter what you face during your journey of life.

Facing the Mirror: My Weight Loss Journey

When I was a young, I felt invisible but also like everyone was looking at me. Imagine going to school in Florida, where it's 95 degrees, and wearing a coat every day just to try and hide how you look. That was me. I struggled with my weight and with feeling good about myself. Kids teased me, and it hurt. My self-esteem was at an all-time low because of the bullying about my weight.

Everything started to change when my mom and I joined Weight Watchers. Together, we learned about healthy eating and how to make better choices. I lost thirty-five pounds. But the weight loss wasn't the only thing that

SELF IMPOERMENT RESET

changed. I learned something powerful: when you surround yourself with individuals who have the same goal and everyone works together, amazing things happen. I also realized that I had control over my actions. That realization made me feel unstoppable. If I could tackle this challenge, what else could I do?

The MBA Challenge: Learning to Think Bigger

A few years earlier, and I was back in the classroom—this time working on my MBA. At first, I only went because my parents encouraged me to. But something changed along the way. I started to take it as a personal challenge to grow and push myself. One class, finance, was especially tough. It wasn't about memorizing answers or picking from multiple-choice questions. Instead, we had to analyze real-world problems, like reading a company's financial statements and explaining what they meant. At first, I struggled because it was really challenging. But this challenge forced me to apply what I was learning in creative ways. It taught me how to think critically, solve problems, and keep pushing even when things got tough. These skills have been critical in my business and personal life. I realized that hard work and inner strength aren't just about working harder—they're about working smarter.

Starting Over: Lessons from Heartbreak

The hardest struggle I've faced came just two months ago. After ten years together, my fiancée and I decided to separate. I wasn't just separating from a relationship—I was leaving behind my family, including two amazing step kids. It felt like a part of who I was, was being ripped away. Holidays, like Thanksgiving, were especially difficult. Everything felt different. But with time, I've come to conclude this change as a chance o grow. I've learned that

SELF IMPOERMENT RESET

even when we're in pain, there's room for new beginnings. Life doesn't end when things get tough; it's just asking us to pivot. The process of letting go helped me focus on gratitude—for the support of my friends, for the lessons my fiancée and I taught each other, and for the chance to start fresh.

One of the most valuable lessons I've learned is this: sometimes we can't see the forest through the trees. But if we trust the process and keep moving forward, we'll come out stronger on the other side.

My Blueprint for Overcoming Challenges

Every challenge I've faced—whether it was losing weight, earning my MBA, or starting over after a long relationship—was an opportunity to grow stronger. Through it all, I developed a blueprint that has helped me move forward and find success, no matter how hard things seemed. I call it my "13 Principles to master Greatness. Let me walk you through the steps:

1. Invest in You: The first step is always investing in yourself. Whether it's joining Weight Watchers, going back to school, or taking a class to learn something new, this principle is the foundation for transformation.

2. Perception is Everything: How you view the world around you matters. When I started really focusing on the good—even in tough times—I found hope and opportunities I didn't know existed.

3. Watch Your Language: The words you use can either build you up or tear you down. I've learned to speak to myself with encouragement and positivity, even when I felt defeated.

SELF IMPOERMENT RESET

4. Discover Your Why: Knowing your purpose gives you the strength to keep going. My "why" has always been about helping others and leaving a positive impact on the world.

5. Visualization is Key: I've always imagined what success looks like before I started working toward it. Whether it was picturing myself healthy, walking across the MBA stage, or thriving after heartbreak, visualization kept me motivated.

6. Create Laser Focus: Life is full of distractions, but focusing on one step at a time is what gets results. I've found that even when things feel overwhelming, breaking goals into smaller pieces makes them manageable.

7. Discipline, Consistency, Balance: This principle has been my compass. Whether it was losing weight or navigating change, staying disciplined and consistent—even when it was hard—was key to success.

8. Goal Setting: You can't hit a target if you don't know what it is. Setting clear, actionable goals helped me measure progress and celebrate small wins along the way.

9. Be in Business for Yourself: While this principle is often about entrepreneurship, it applies to our life too. Taking ownership of your goals and being accountable for your actions is a game-changer.

10. Networking &amp; Giving: I wouldn't be where I am without the support of others. Surrounding myself with people who lifted me up—and giving back to those in need—created a cycle of positivity and success.

11. Track It: Finances; Health: Keeping track of what is important—whether it's what you eat, your exercise habits, or your spending—keeps you in control and moving toward your goals.

12. 10X Everything: When I was stuck, I realized I wasn't aiming high enough. Dreaming bigger and putting in ten times the effort. It all made all the difference in reaching my goals.

13. Plan. Do. Review.: This principle ties it all together. Every time I face a challenge, I create a plan, take action, and reflect on what worked and what didn't. This cycle of improvement keeps me growing.

These principles aren't just ideas—they're practical steps you can apply to any challenge in your life. Whether you're losing weight, starting a new career, or rebuilding after loss, this blueprint can guide you forward.

Inner Peace: A Work in Progress

For me, inner peace isn't about having a perfect life. It's about knowing I did my best with the time I had each day. It's about focusing on what fulfills me, like helping others and being part of something bigger than myself. When I think about the legacy I want to leave behind, it motivates me to keep going, no matter how rocky the road gets.

If you're going through a tough time, remember this: You're not alone. Whether you're struggling with weight, school, or relationships, there's always a way forward. Believe in yourself—or borrow someone else's belief in you until you can believe in yourself. Like Les Brown says, "You have greatness within you."

SELF IMPOERMENT RESET

Closing Thoughts: Start Today

No matter where you are in your life, just know that it's okay to start over. Every challenge is a chance to grow. It might not feel like it now, but one day you'll look back and see how far you've come. Take it one step at a time, lean on others when you need to, and never stop believing in all the possibilities around you.

SELF IMPOERMENT RESET

~ Brendan McCauley ~

Brendan McCauley is an international best-selling author and systems expert on a mission to empower coaches and business owners to streamline their operations and scale their impact. With an MBA and over a decade of entrepreneurial experience, Brendan specializes in creating simple, effective solutions that help others achieve their goals.

Connect with him on Facebook:

at https://www.facebook.com/officialbrendanm or explore his CRM solutions at https://crmdonebetter.com.

SELF IMPOERMENT RESET

Chapter 15

~ Lulwa Saffarini ~

Finally Free

When you have been tortured by silence, you can not help but feel it in your bones. Like the world withholding. Like life withdrawing. Quiet. Never at peace, but quiet. Quiet …. Be
QUIET……………………………………………………..

The room was buzzing as usual with family merriment and conversation, loud animated voices speaking to each other and over each other and filling the room with laughter, heated arguments and family gossip. My mom sat in a corner chair, looking forlorn - a picture of stoic sorrow. As the apple of my grandfather's eye, naturally, he noticed first and asked: "baba, what's going on with you?" "Nothing," she said. He looked uneasy, probed again, and got the same answer, and so left it at that while giving my grandmother an inquisitive look, which very quickly ping ponged between every adult.

The room hushed for a few minutes, and gradually, the volume increased, nearly returning to its previous energetic normal. "Did I tell you what Asaad did for me on my birthday? The sweetest thing!" gushed my aunt, sneaking a quick look at my mom, muting her laughter as if ashamed of her happiness. Almost back to normal, but not quite. The awkward pauses increased ever so slightly; the joyous, carefree conversations were damped by the furtive glances and pensive eyes.

SELF IMPOERMENT RESET

"Arafat was a shrewd politician. He kept the pack of vultures around him in check, yes, he bribed them, but judiciously so, and he never took a penny for himself, not something you can say about any of the Arab leaders," declared her husband. "Nonsense. There is no such thing. By the small corruption he entertained, he opened the door for more," bellowed my uncle. My mom sighed with sadness. "Ya mama ya habibti, what's up? We are concerned," said my grandmother "Nothing," whispered my mom. "You can't stay like this mama, staring sadly in the distance when you are with family," she shrieked emphatically. "Leave her alone," scolded my grandfather, his voice landing like a muted thud.

The silence dragged on, longer this time, awkward concern and indecision hung in the air. And again, the rhythm slowly picked up, accelerating and the damp darkness was lifting again. Political debates, stories about the sordid behavior of colleagues and family members resumed. Almost back to normal, but not quite. Awkward pauses, Muted joy, Indecisive glances, my mom sighed… louder this time, and a tear rolled down her cheek. Quiet, the room went oh so quiet but not at peace, never at peace. The absence of sound, brought to life through tension, at once silent and high strung. "Habibti baba inti, why are you upset? I will break the skull of whoever upset you," my grandfather spoke, directing his words to my mom and his eyes filling up with tears. "Please mama, please tell us. We will not allow this to continue. Your sadness lands heavy on my chest ya mama," my grandmother's voice quivered unnaturally.

All at once, everyone began speaking, yelling, begging…. Please, say something! Frantic anxiety turned fully grown adults into children, willing to do anything to STOP THE

SELF IMPOERMENT RESET

SILENCE, the quiet that beats louder than a drum. Wherever my mom went, she brought quiet time with her. She wielded QUIET like a weapon.

    The stage was set. Silence had primed all, and they were finally ready for sound. And so, she blurted out: "Lulwa" The crackling energy in the room turned towards me. And all at once, everyone looked at me with accusation, anger, and aggression. All at once, everyone started speaking, yelling, pointing. "What did you do this time?!" "Why are you always so difficult?" "Why do you torture your mother so?!!!" "What did your mom do to deserve a child like you?" Hysteria…

    When an insatiable need to be heard hits the wall of futility. When all the words in the world barrel down, needing to be spoken, all at once, and in the process trample each other to death…. Like a crazed crowd turning into a full-blown riot. I screamed… with hysteria. QUIET won. She won…
again……………………………………………………………..

    For as long as I remember, I knew QUIET… intimately, we had a very special and sticky kind of relationship. She was the overlord. I was the underling. She was cold. She was cruel. She was the restraint, control, and precision of a master war strategist. She was the queen dominatrix, administering colossal conquest… without heart. I despised her. I revered her.

    In my interior world, quiet was LOUD. When she showed up, my whole world trembled. I was feeble, frayed, frazzled, and fantastically out of control. I was a flurry of sound without sense. When she appeared, I crumbled, fell apart and EXPLODED. Like a sonic bomb without a

SELF IMPOERMENT RESET

center. I loathed myself, for who I was when QUIET made her presence known disgusted me.

You know you've been infected by QUIET when every moment unoccupied by words or activity spells danger. You know you are under her spell when the gaps between messages, calls, or dates with someone you are into fill you with terror, and you react, with a gnarly neediness. You promise you won't, but eventually…you WILL react, of that you and I are both certain. And though you pretend it is nothing, your insides tell you, it is everything. You know you've been poisoned when you would rather blow up 10 years of marriage than withstand a request to pause and take space in the middle of an argument. You know you're at her mercy when the withdrawal of someone, anyone, even those you despise compels you to reach out and close the gap - at the expense of your boundaries, bandwidth and very

BEING.

You know you're lost to the QUIET when your thoughts can never rest, when you pack your calendar down to the last minute with "doings," and when you cannot be still when everything within and without you is in flux….

For as long as I remember, my deepest desire was to become the overlord, to wield QUIET like a consummate mistress. I would lie down in bed, face up right before I fell asleep every night, conjuring her up, restrained, composed and ice cold. It was a fervent fantasy, one that I never really believed I would attain, and it would have remained so had it not been for my life undergoing complete combustion. In a little over a year, I moved continents, ended a marriage, lost my homebase - my friends & family, and the ecosystem I've built to support me, got

SELF IMPOERMENT RESET

fired and spent all my savings, right in the middle of the pandemic.

I lost everything and found the Modern Mystery School. I found myself sitting across from my now guide, Christina Becerra, as I talked, and talked, and talked some more… for over an hour and a half without pause. My thoughts were like a thousand shards of glass spilling out of my mouth incoherently and with great emotion. She listened, and listened, and listened some more. With intent. With presence. Without pitying, blaming, judging, or advising. She listened, with divine quiet.

My soul soaked up quiet, it rounded the jagged edges of my broken thoughts. It stilled the roiling of my tumultuous emotions. It brought me back to myself. In retrospect, I believe my spirit remembered quiet. It was unlike anything I have ever experienced before, and yet so familiar, like coming home for the first time and finding traces of myself in every corner, my perfume hanging in the air, and the book I'm reading opening onto the page where I last left it. I trusted her that day because I trusted the quiet in her.

I stepped onto the path, and received a series of initiations, activations, and healings. With every step on the path, I was initiated into God's quiet. The quiet that holds. The quiet that settles onto your core like the warm sun of an early summer morning. The quiet that packs stability into your every bone and sinew. That quiet grew and grew, until one day I had an experience that left me knowing without doubt that if I wanted to, I could be the overlord; I could wield QUIET like a weapon.

I was tempted, but only a little because in my journey I found what is unexpectedly better… You know you've found quiet when the chirping birds sing into your very

SELF IMPOERMENT RESET

cells and your whole-body thrums with their trills, when you wake up to the sunrise and its beauty stuns you into submission, and the colors sound like an angelic symphony. You know you've been initiated into her grace when you can be in the middle of the most heated fight, when you can feel the heat of your emotions revving up, and the activity of the mind and still anchor into the solidity of your quiet center.

You know you've been brought into her innermost temple when you are filled to the brim with the aliveness of her BEING, and the expansive spaciousness of her endless shores, when quiet spills over with joy, and pours into doing, as if compelled to create, if only to express this beauty……………………………………………………."You are my daughter, I love you", whispered my mom as I nestled into her. We listened in quiet to A Vava Inouva by Idir.

It took me forty years to come into my mom's special brand of divine quiet, to share in the glorious light of her inner radiance, to settle into a quiet seeing that perceives the God-spark within her, that only she can gift the world with. Beyond right and wrong, Outside the confines of victim and villain, When I stopped being the underling, and ceased to crave the power of the overlord. In the spacious expanse of inner peace, where only God's LIGHT shines.

I was finally free; we were finally free!

SELF IMPOERMENT RESET

~ Lulwa Saffarini ~

For nearly 20 years, Lulwa has built networks and communities of purpose worldwide. She convened governments, businesses, financiers, and communities to create transformative initiatives, such as:

- Establishing a humanitarian network spanning 10 countries.
- Powering villages with solar energy.
- Providing towns with clean water.
- Launching ecotourism destinations serving tens of thousands annually.

That is... until she lost everything and realized she'd never built a deep in-dwelling sense of place within. As an initiate in King Solomon's lineage with the Modern Mystery School, she discovered that Bardo — the in-between where what "*was*" is gone and what "*will be*" is not yet — is where all power resides. Spiritual masters have long known this: Bardo is a portal for EXPANSION.

She founded Bardo Transformation, a spiritually rooted wellness company dedicated to helping people going through major life transitions.

Reclaim Power. Reinvent Themselves. Reimagine Possibilities. Rebuild Life.

.www.bardotransformation.com

Instagram: bardotransformation
(https://www.instagram.com/bardotransformation/profilecard/?igsh=MWE0ZGJjazZzdWQzYw==)

LinkedIn: https://www.linkedin.com/in/lulwa-saffarini-46baa564

~ Chapter 16 ~

Denise Millett Burkhardt

Displayed Separation

I would love to take this opportunity to share a story about someone very near to me and I know it reflets self-empowerment and the rocky road to inner peace because it is so raw and deep that only God could bring a sense of calm under the circumstances. A young mother lost her husband to murder, and she had a son with the love of her life. When the murder happened the worlds of both of them were forever upended into turmoil.

The loss was too much in itself, but the wounds would be opened more and more as extreme loss came into play. The grandparents of the child from the father's side immediately swept into action, playing on the grief and loss of the mother and took custody of her son. As if all of this was not devastating enough, she mourned and grieved in only ways that a mother with such a loss could understand.

Upon taking custody of the child, the grandparents became disenchanted with the responsibility and care of the child and sent him to a mental facility. This only brought more distraught and grieving and intense pain to the mother and the child. The separation was unbearable, but the young mother held strong and found others to help her in finding out where her son was placed.

SELF IMPOERMENT RESET

   Once she found out, she learned that there was intense abuse happening within the facility and that they were giving him puberty blockers and telling him that he was actually a girl. He faced brutal treatment throughout his childhood years and the state had full custody of the child because of the choice the grandparents had made.

   Through the years the young mother, stricken with grief, she tried and tried to find any way hat she could get her child back. Years later, (At 15 years old- this is how long this went on) the child ran away from the facility and an investigator was hired who found the young man and returned him to his mother. The length of time that he had been there created more mental issues and barriers for his mental health. Yes, they were reunited, but many issues had to be worked through for healing on both sides. Some things just never go away.

   The truth is that God sustained both of them throughout the years of displacement and separation. The young man used drugs to medicate and overcome the pain that he felt and ran away often.

   The fact that abuse is running rampant in our mental health facilities is atrocious and we also have seen in the recent days how trafficking has been a bigger issue than anyone could have imagined.

   Through counseling and prayer, the two have come together over the years and have experienced joy, grief, more pain, and lots of growth. It has not been easy. Throughout the transition, the young man received opportunities to get an education, work and become a contributing citizen in his community. Years later, he met someone whom he loved, and they had a beautiful daughter together.

SELF IMPOERMENT RESET

I just want to take a moment and say that it is not easy to come from trauma and see a happy ending. There are people who are using drugs and abused and seeking God in their lives by the millions every single day. Only the strong survive, but GOD is mindful of all of us. I know this from the bottom of my heart. With God, nothing is impossible. Those who are suffering he will bring justice, and he will mind his flock. I have seen incredible growth and maturity and healing and love and compassion through this experience of this incredible woman. She is a rock. Stellar and strong. She has felt the worse of pain and loss that I could ever imagine.

The road to inner peace can be short or long depending upon the trauma or stress that is in one's life. One day at a time can look like one minute at a time. Even one second at a time in some extreme situations. But being patient, having faith in God, never giving up and pouring out tearful prayer to a God who is miraculous is the biggest proof of his everlasting love. The road to inner peace is different for everyone. No two stories are the same and each one is unique and just as important and meaningful as the other. Your story and your suffering could be the strength that someone else finds just by hearing it. You are the only one who can make a difference.

When you have hard experiences in your life, how do you move through them? Do you hide and feel anxious? Are you grieving so that you have to medicate or other means to deal and cope with the pain? There are so many moving parts to a traumatic experience that can take years to come to a head and then years to even heal. Some of the treasures I have found over the years are prayer, meditation, deep faith, deep hope, and unconditional love. As I have watched this young woman through the last few

SELF IMPOERMENT RESET

decades of her life, I have noted the maturity and the strength that she has pulled within herself to endure to the end. She, at one point, saw no end to her pain. She, at one point, saw no relief, no shelter for her pain, and no support to fix the situation. It had to unravel itself through a very, very long process.

She became empowered by taking it a day at a time and showing incredible faith and trust in a God that could only be the one to heal both herself and her son. I might add it is still a work in the process, but the road for her inner peace has taken years and years. As life goes on and maturity comes into play, I see a strong and powerful warrior who can show unconditional love and kindness to everyone around her.

Please have faith in the process. Please use your prayers and believe that inner peace can be found. Use meditation, others who are there to support you, and take care of yourself when it is out of your control. I promise you the journey is not the destination. It is the experience, no matter the pain or joy, that ALWAYS comes full circle.

God Bless You All.

SELF IMPOERMENT RESET

~ Denise Millett Burkhardt ~

Denise Millett Burkhardt was born and raised in Brooklyn, New York, and received a congressional award for her invaluable service to the community. She also received the "Producer's Award" from the Mayor of Los Angeles for being multicultural and making the city a better place to live and work. The youngest woman ever to own an OTT Networks, Denise has given away over twelve million charitable dollars airtime on fourteen Networks, and now has a platform, Traverse TV, that will be a basis for positive reinforcement through music, entertainment, health, nutrition education, and information. All rated PG-14 reaching a global audience. Denise is working on a project to house 30-40,000 homeless Veterans and end the homeless population by the year 2030 by duplicating every program in the State. Very soon, she will be rolling out a K-12 Global Educational Program that will pay students in Crypto Currency to learn and get a better overall education through Satellite Delivery. She will also be launching a Worldwide Tele-Medicine Platform through Satellite Delivery that will provide unlimited options for medical care.

denisemb@traversetv.com

~ Chapter 17 ~

Linda McBee

Tools for Overcoming Life's Challenges

Life is filled with unexpected twists and turns, moments when everything feels as though .it is unravelling at once. These experiences—whether personal, professional, or emotional—can shake us to the core. They often leave us wondering how to navigate through the storm and come out whole on the other side. In my journey, the road to inner peace has been anything but smooth. There have been times when I felt utterly unprepared for the challenges life threw my way. Like many of us, I didn't always have the tools or the wisdom to handle adversity with grace. But along the way, I've been fortunate to learn strategies that helped me not only survive life's curveballs but also grow from them. It is my hope that by sharing these tools, you too can find the resilience and strength to face life's challenges while cultivating peace within yourself.

When my dog, Honey, passed away a few months ago, I felt completely unmoored. In my grief, I instinctively reached for my favorite journal and pen, pouring out thoughts and emotions that I could not process. As I wrote, I began to realize something profound: dogs are incredible gifts to us. They help us heal in ways we might never anticipate. Honey was no exception. The walks we took, the journeys we shared, and the people she brought into our lives—all of it shaped the path I was unknowingly traveling. Even now, those who met her still talk about her, sharing in the loss my husband and I feel.

Looking back, I see now that the seven years Honey spent with us were part of my own healing journey. Her presence, her love, and even her quiet patience helped me navigate the rocky road to inner peace. I did not fully understand her purpose until she was gone, but I'm certain now that she had one—a mission to guide me. She found me through a friend who noticed her unique connection to me. Every time I visited, Honey would cry as if she knew we were meant to be together. Though I'm allergic to dogs, she somehow sensed that and would gently nudge me for hugs instead of licking me. My husband met her once, and she leapt into his truck without hesitation, immediately claiming him as hers. I sometimes wonder if she saw the connection between us before we even realized it ourselves. Honey didn't just teach me how to find peace—she helped me heal the wounds of my inner child. She became both a teacher and a companion, leading me toward a deeper understanding of myself. Her lessons remain with me, and they've inspired me to share the tools I used to continue on the journey she started. Do you have an animal in your life nudging you to dig deeper, heal, and find your own inner peace?

1. Journaling: A Path to Self-Discovery

One of the most transformative tools I've adopted is journaling. Writing has become a way to process my emotions, confront my fears, and better understand myself. In moments of chaos, journaling serves as a grounding practice, helping me sort through the thoughts and feelings that can otherwise feel overwhelming.

SELF IMPOERMENT RESET

Journaling offers several benefits:

☐ **Emotional release**: Writing provides a safe space to express feelings that are difficult to share out loud.

☐ **Clarity:** By putting thoughts on paper, you can often see patterns or solutions that weren't apparent before.

☐ **Healing**: Reflecting on your experiences allows you to process pain and move toward acceptance.

For me, journaling became especially important during a season of deep grief. The simple act of writing helped me explore the depths of my sadness, giving me the courage to face it head-on. Over time, I began to uncover lessons and insights that gave me strength for the road ahead.

2. Walking in Nature: Reconnecting with the Earth

There is something inherently healing about spending time in nature. The fresh air, the sunlight, and the quiet presence of the natural world have a way of soothing the mind and body. For me, walking in nature has become a sacred ritual—a time to step away from the busyness of life and reconnect with the simplicity of creation.

Walking outdoors has numerous benefits:

☐ **Physical rejuvenation**: The movement itself boosts energy and reduces stress.

☐ **Mental clarity**: Being surrounded by nature fosters mindfulness and helps you focus on the present moment.

☐ **Spiritual connection**: Nature often reminds us of life's beauty and the abundance of creation. On particularly stressful days, I find that even a short walk can shift my perspective. The rhythm of my steps, the feel of the sun on

SELF IMPOERMENT RESET

my skin, and the sound of the wind in the trees remind me that life is bigger than the challenges I face.

3. Meditation and Prayer: Finding Stillness

When life feels overwhelming, it's easy to get caught up in the noise—both external and internal. Meditation and prayer have been invaluable practices for quieting my mind and reconnecting with what truly matters.

Meditation doesn't require perfection or even total silence. For me, it's as simple as sitting in stillness, focusing on my breath, and allowing my thoughts to settle. This practice creates space to reflect and listen to my inner voice. Prayer, on the other hand, is my way of seeking guidance and comfort. It's where I pour out my worries and find reassurance that I'm not walking this road alone. Together, meditation and prayer provide a sense of calm that allows me to approach challenges with greater clarity and strength.

4. Self-Care: Honoring the Body and Mind

During difficult times, self-care becomes more than a luxury—it's a necessity. Taking care of ourselves physically, mentally, and emotionally is essential for resilience. Over the years, I've discovered that self-care isn't just about indulgence; it's about restoration and balance.

Here are a few self-care practices that have been especially meaningful to me:

☐ **Hot baths**: A warm bath with Epsom salts, baking soda, and essential oils can do wonders for the body and mind. It's a simple but powerful way to relax and release tension.

☐ **Nourishing foods:** Eating whole, natural foods helps me feel grounded and energized. I often turn to fresh

SELF IMPOERMENT RESET

vegetables, fruits, and herbal teas to restore balance during stressful periods.

☐ **Rest: Prioritizing** sleep and downtime is crucial for maintaining strength and focus. Self-care is a way of reminding ourselves that we are worthy of kindness and attention—even from ourselves.

5. Creativity: Healing Through Expression

Creativity has been one of the most surprising tools on my journey to inner peace. Whether it's cooking, painting, writing, or trying a new hobby, creative expression allows us to channel emotions into something meaningful. For me, cooking has been an especially therapeutic outlet. Preparing a meal is not just about feeding the body—it's about nourishing the soul. The process of experimenting with new recipes and creating something beautiful from simple ingredients reminds me of life's possibilities. Creativity is a reminder that even in the midst of difficulty, there is room for joy, exploration, and growth.

Embracing Adversity as a Teacher

One of the greatest lessons I've learned on my rocky road to inner peace is that adversity, though painful, can be a powerful teacher. It forces us to grow in ways we never anticipated, deepening our resilience, and strengthening our character. Challenges teach us patience, humility, and the importance of leaning on others when we need support. They remind us that we don't have to carry our burdens alone. I've also learned that adversity often reveals our inner strength—the strength we didn't realize we had until we were forced to use it. While the road may be difficult, each step we take brings us closer to a deeper understanding of ourselves and the peace we seek.

SELF IMPOERMENT RESET

The Ongoing Journey

Finding inner peace is not a destination; it's an ongoing process. Life will always present us with new challenges, but with the right tools, we can face them with grace and resilience. Journaling, walking in nature, meditation, self-care, and creativity are just a few of the practices that have helped me on my journey. They serve as reminders that even in our darkest moments, we have the power to heal, grow, and find joy. While the road to inner peace may be rocky, it is also rich with lessons, growth, and unexpected beauty. By embracing the journey, we open ourselves to the possibility of transformation and discover the strength that lies within us.

SELF IMPOERMENT RESET

~ Linda McBee ~

Linda McBee has a degree in Psychology with n emphasis on Mental Health, as she is Therapist. She has been educating people about finance, marketing, and health for fifty years and continues to help people with their health today. She got her Functional Medicine Coaching Certification in order to take someone's health to the next level, also! Her mantra is "Health is Wealth!" without your health, you do not anything… take it from her experience! She would be happy to share more of her story with you. She now helps people get healthy with a candy that is super easy and affordable! Stop choking down tablets that are making you sicker and that your body is rejecting.

Happy DNA Candy, 443-744-0001

http://HappyDNACandy.com

SELF IMPOERMENT RESET

~ Acknowledgments ~

Thank you too my higher self for guiding me through this very interesting Journey called life. I have learned to trust my higher self as that part of me is the most intuitive and knows what I need.
My higher self is basically a team of angels trying to keep me out of trouble most of the time.

This amazing collaborative book is put together to help people who are going through their own mud and trying to swim through it. I'm working so hard like I don't have to do that now they hit a doping me we are here to tell you that we too have gone through the mud and survived and to let you know that this too shall pass. I believe in my heart of hearts that we go through the mud so that we know what the good times are we know when we've succeeded, and I hate to sound cliche, but all your hard work leads to Greatness. I thought oh my God he's right especially if you want to be a coach and more especially if you want to be an entrepreneur. When you work for yourself, you have no one else to blame so then you have to come eye to eye with your own self and figure out how am I going to get out of this mess all by myself. You can certainly ask for help still but the opportunity does not present itself for you to blame someone else you, have to come eye to eye with yourself and deal with yourself. This, for sure, is not the path of least resistance.
Thank you for sharing our journey with us. Life is great!

LOVE +LIGHT!
Dr. Rev. MARIANNE

SELF IMPOERMENT RESET

SELF IMPOERMENT RESET

SELF IMPOERMENT RESET

SELF IMPOERMENT RESET